Author's Note

The contents of the writing were copied from Chapters 21 and 50 of the book "Ares Le Mandat" written by Anthony of Boston, who is the same author of this book.

**A Book that Could Make a Bitcoin Trader
Wealthy Overnight:**

**Day trading and Macro Prediction Algorithms for Bitcoin using
Astrological-based techniques and methods**

Anthony of Boston

Bitcoin Research Prediction Algorithms

In the next example using Bitcoin(BTC/USD), we have a different algorithm with a different set of parameters and also 2 sets of parameter. Once again, the predictions apply to where the value of Bitcoin finishes relative to the day before.

In these examples we will have 2 sets of 9 parameters based on Eclipses360 to see how it correlates to the daily Bitcoin(BTC/USD) movements. This is a much more complicated algorithm and is likely a hint to the mark of the beast economy. In my studies there seems to be something taking place when the Sun and Mercury changes relationship to each other. It seems as though whatever is applied during the time when the degree of mercury is less than the degree of the sun in any sign is exactly the opposite of what happens when the degree of mercury is more than the degree of the sun in any sign. That change in the relationship between the sun and mercury seems to change the outcome of the applied algorithm.

The algorithm is made up 2 sets of parameters defined to predict the movements of the BTC/USD. See the next page for the first set of parameters.

These "**Figure Set 1**" parameters only apply when the degree of mercury is **less** than the degree of the sun.

Note: Keep these pages of "Figure Set 1" referenced to see how the parameters correlate to past Bitcoin prices in the upcoming examples

Figure Set 1

1. When the moon is within 1 degree of the degree of the sun in an Earth or Water sign, the value of Bitcoin(BTC/USD) tends to go up. For instance, the zodiac goes as follows: **aries, taurus, gemini, cancer, leo, virgo, libra, scorpio, sagittarius, capricorn, aquarius, and pisces**. The Earth and Water signs are Taurus, Cancer, Virgo, Scorpio, Capricorn, and Pisces. .

2. When the moon is within 1 degree of the degree of the sun in an Fire or Air sign, the value of Bitcoin(BTC/USD) tends to go down. For instance, the zodiac goes as follows: **aries, taurus, gemini, cancer, leo, virgo, libra, scorpio, sagittarius, capricorn, aquarius, and pisces**. The Fire and Air signs are Aries, Gemini, Leo, Libra, Sagittarius, Aquarius.

3. When the moon is within 3 degrees of the degree of the lunar node in any sign, the result is that the value of Bitcoin(BTC/USD) drops.

4. when the moon is within 1 degree of the degree of the lunar node after the moon has passed the degree of the sun in an Earth or Water sign, Bitcoin's(BTC/USD) value tends to drop.

5. when the moon is within 1 degree of the degree of the lunar node after the moon has passed the degree of the sun in a Fire or Air sign, Bitcoin's(BTC/USD) value tends to rise.

6. When moon is within 3 degrees of the degree of the Sun in an Earth or Water sign, Bitcoin's(BTC/USD) value tends to drop.

7. When the moon is within 3 degrees of the degree of the Sun in a Fire or Air sign, Bitcoin(BTC/USD) tends to rise.

8. When the moon is within 1 degree of the degree of the Mercury after the moon has passed the degree of the sun in an Earth or Water sign, Bitcoin's(BTC/USD) value tends to drop.

9. When the moon is within 1 degree of the degree of Mercury after the moon has passed the degree of the sun in a Fire or Air sign, the Bitcoin's(BTC/USD) value tends to rise.

Figure Set 2 starts on the next page

Keep the pages of "Figure Set 2" referenced to see how the parameters correlate to past Bitcoin prices in the upcoming examples

These "**Figure Set 2**" parameters only apply when the degree of mercury is **greater** than the degree of the sun.

Figure Set 2

1. When the moon is within 1 degree of the degree of the sun in an Earth or Water sign, the value of Bitcoin(BTC/USD) tends to go down. For instance, the zodiac goes as follows: **aries, taurus, gemini, cancer, leo, virgo, libra, scorpio, sagittarius, capricorn, aquarius, and pisces**. The Earth and Water signs are Taurus, Cancer, Virgo, Scorpio, Capricorn, and Pisces. .

2. When the moon is within 1 degree of the degree of the sun in an Fire or Air sign, the value of Bitcoin(BTC/USD) tends to go up. For instance, the zodiac goes as follows: **aries, taurus, gemini, cancer, leo, virgo, libra, scorpio, sagittarius, capricorn, aquarius, and pisces**. The Fire and Air signs are Aries, Gemini, Leo, Libra, Sagittarius, Aquarius.

3. When the moon is within 3 degrees of the degree of the lunar node in any sign, the result is that the value of Bitcoin(BTC/USD) drops.

4. when the moon is within 1 degree of the degree of the lunar node after the moon has passed the degree of the sun in an Earth or Water sign, Bitcoin's(BTC/USD) value tends to rise.

5. when the moon is within 1 degree of the degree of the lunar node after the moon has passed the degree of the sun in a Fire or Air sign, Bitcoin's(BTC/USD) value tends to drop.

6. When moon is within 3 degrees of the degree of the Sun in an Earth or Water sign, Bitcoin's(BTC/USD) value tends to rise.

Figure Set 2 cont'd

7. When the moon is within 3 degrees of the degree of the Sun in a Fire or Air sign, Bitcoin(BTC/USD) tends to drop.

8. When the moon is within 1 degree of the degree of the Mercury after the moon has passed the degree of the sun in an Earth or Water sign, the Bitcoin's(BTC/USD) value tends to rise.

9. When the moon is within 1 degree of the degree of the Mercury after the moon has passed the degree of the sun in a Fire or Air sign, the Bitcoin's(BTC/USD) value tends to drop.

Go to the next page to see how these parameters apply to trading.

Bitcoin/USD

Date	Price	Open	High	Low	Vol.	Change %
Jan 31, 2014	800.0	801.7	803.3	791.8	0.22K	-0.49%
Jan 30, 2014	803.9	794.4	803.9	785.4	0.27K	0.49%
Jan 29, 2014	800.0	789.0	800.0	783.6	0.13K	0.63%
Jan 28, 2014	795.0	779.8	812.0	770.0	0.56K	4.57%
Jan 27, 2014	760.3	810.9	810.9	757.0	0.74K	-6.10%
Jan 26, 2014	809.7	804.2	823.9	731.0	0.15K	-0.04%
Jan 25, 2014	810.0	795.8	810.0	789.4	0.23K	3.60%
Jan 24, 2014	781.9	800.0	800.0	773.2	0.36K	-4.21%
Jan 23, 2014	816.2	819.0	820.0	804.3	0.26K	1.14%
Jan 22, 2014	807.0	807.0	807.0	807.0	0.00K	-0.37%
Jan 21, 2014	810.0	810.0	824.7	794.2	0.37K	-1.62%
Jan 20, 2014	823.4	831.0	831.0	795.2	0.15K	-0.80%
Jan 19, 2014	830.0	819.0	830.0	814.2	0.14K	3.75%
Jan 18, 2014	800.0	810.0	815.0	799.0	0.15K	1.39%
Jan 17, 2014	789.0	820.0	820.7	789.0	0.07K	-4.25%
Jan 16, 2014	824.0	847.1	847.1	822.4	0.20K	-1.87%
Jan 15, 2014	839.7	835.5	842.2	833.7	0.05K	1.56%
Jan 14, 2014	826.9	827.8	833.4	815.1	0.14K	1.03%
Jan 13, 2014	818.4	846.6	857.3	818.4	0.06K	-7.85%
Jan 12, 2014	888.1	892.0	892.0	888.1	0.00K	-0.98%
Jan 11, 2014	896.9	899.0	900.3	895.0	0.01K	7.44%
Jan 10, 2014	834.7	833.0	834.7	833.0	0.00K	-1.79%
Jan 09, 2014	850.0	833.7	850.0	794.9	0.29K	2.59%
Jan 08, 2014	828.5	781.0	838.0	771.0	0.14K	4.75%
Jan 07, 2014	791.0	928.7	928.7	791.0	0.10K	-15.36%
Jan 06, 2014	934.5	910.0	950.0	900.0	0.10K	3.38%
Jan 05, 2014	904.0	839.5	904.0	839.5	0.02K	12.74%
Jan 04, 2014	801.8	806.5	806.5	801.8	0.01K	-1.26%
Jan 03, 2014	812.1	801.0	812.1	801.0	-	4.78%
Jan 02, 2014	775.0	746.2	775.0	740.2	0.13K	4.69%
Jan 01, 2014	740.3	740.0	757.0	733.5	0.01K	1.73%

Highest: 950.0   Lowest: 731.0   Difference: 219.0   Average: 819.4   Change %: 9.9

These are the prices for the BTC/USD for the month of January 2014

We will use January, February and early March of 2014 in our example for Bitcoin's value correlating with Eclipses. **Remember**: we have 2 sets of parameters for this Bitcoin algorithm: Figure Set 1 and Figure Set 2. Both are based on the relationship between the degree of the sun and the degree of mercury. **Figure Set 1** applies when the degree of mercury is less than the degree of the sun, while **Figure Set 2** applies when the degree of mercury is greater than the degree of the sun. So lets start with January. On January 1st, 2nd, and 3rd , BTC/USD's value rose all three days. See the chart on the next page. Please note: Figure Set 1 and Figure Set 2 are basically the opposite of each other, with the exception of parameter 3. That one is the same in both.

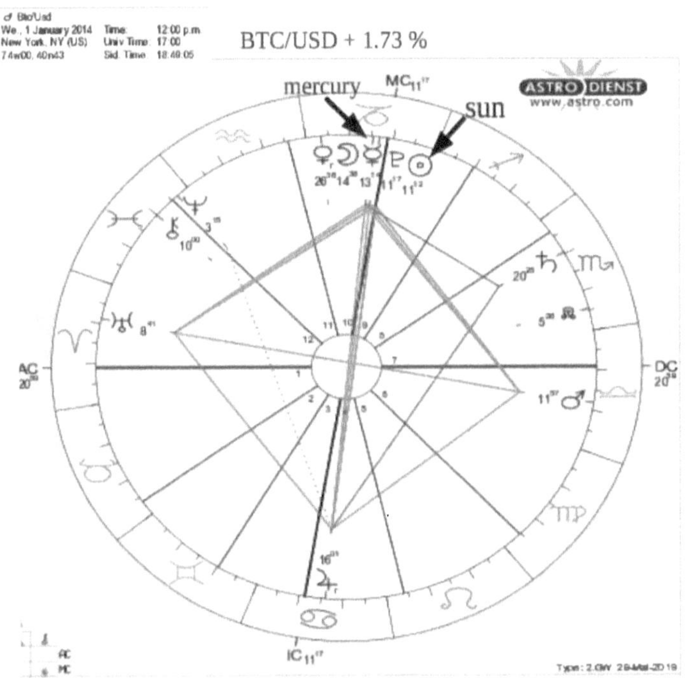

Since we have 2 sets of parameters for this algorithm, we have to see which set do we apply here. We do that by looking at the relationship between the degree of the sun and the degree of mercury. In this chart for January 1st 2014, mercury is at 13 degrees and the sun is at 11 degrees. Therefore, the degree of mercury is higher than the sun's degree. So that means we use **"Figure Set 2"** parameters to asses where BTC/USD would go this day. Just go back to the page where the **Figure Set 2** parameters are laid out. The last parameter that applies in this chart would be parameter 8 which says the moon being within 1 degree of the degree of the Mercury after the moon has passed the degree of the sun in an Earth or Water sign makes the value of BTC/USD to go up. The sun is in capricorn, so the moon having been within 1 degree of the degree of mercury becomes defined by the fact that the sun's degree is in an Earth sign. So the parameter's prediction is correct. BTC/USD was up + 1.73%

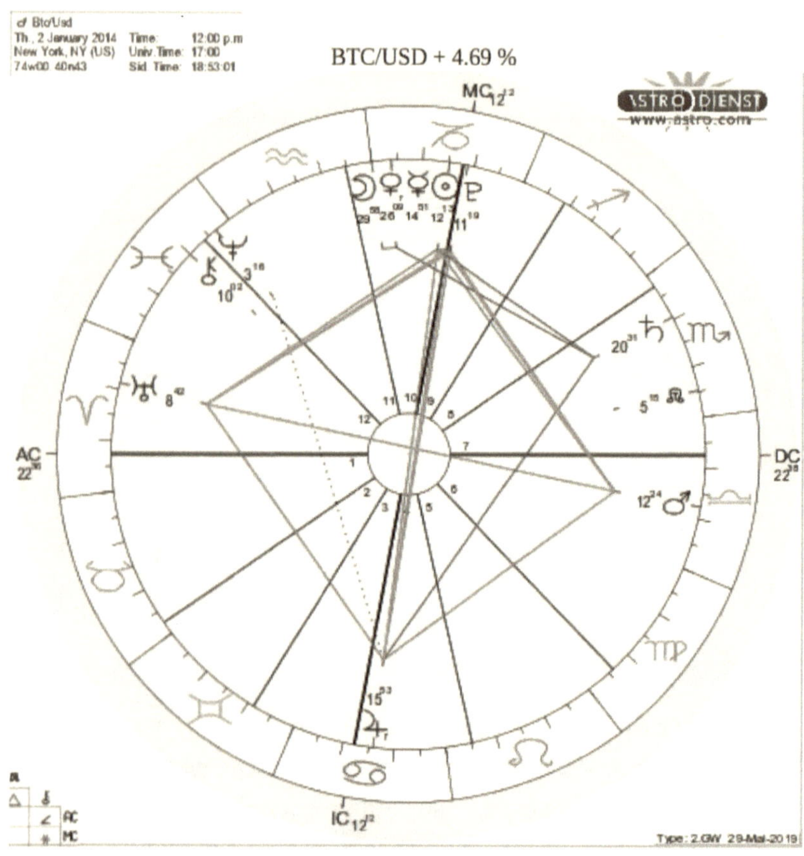

In this chart for Jan 2 2014, the degree of mercury is still higher than the sun's degree, so the **"Figure Set 2"** parameters still apply. When looking at the chart, the last parameter that would have applied from **"Figure Set 2"** would be parameter 8 again. The moon being within 1 degree of the degree of mercury with the degree of the sun being in an earth or water sign is defined to bring the value of BTC/USD up. The BTC/USD was up +4.69% that day.

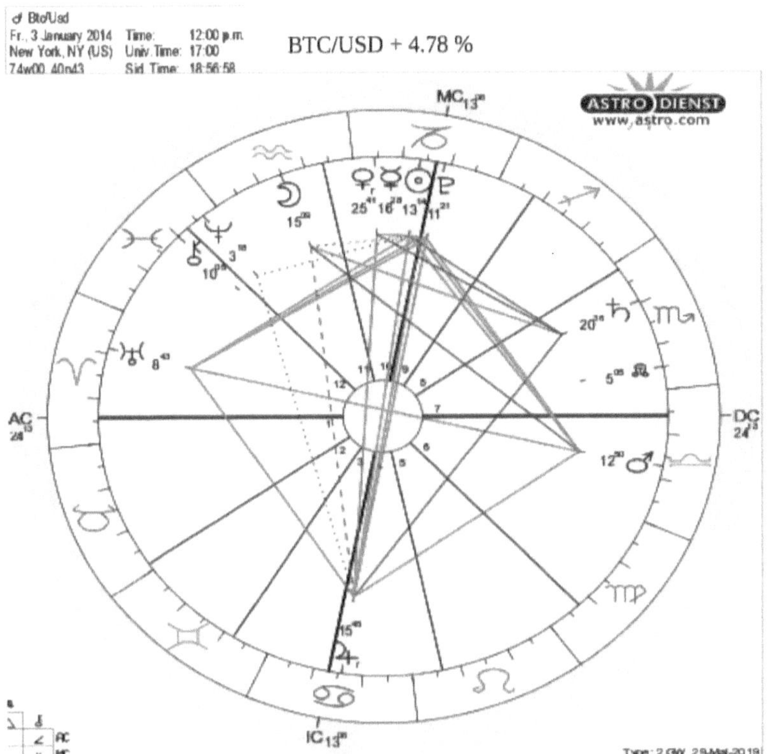

In this chart for Jan 3, 2014, the degree of mercury(16 degrees) is still higher than the sun's degree(13 degrees), so the **"Figure Set 2"** parameters still apply here. When looking at the chart, the last parameter that would have applied from **"Figure Set 2"** would be parameter 2, which says the moon being within 1 degree of the degree of the sun in a fire or air sign brings the value of BTC/USD up. That moon is in Aquarius and the parameter 2 would have occurred in Aquarius, an air sign. The BTC/USD was up +4.78% this day. Its important to notice that with the moon at 15^{09} degrees and almost exactly within 1 degree of the degree of mercury(which is 16^{28} degrees), its close to its next parameter that describes what happens when the moon is within 1 degree of the degree of mercury after the moon has passed the degree of the sun in an air or fire sign.

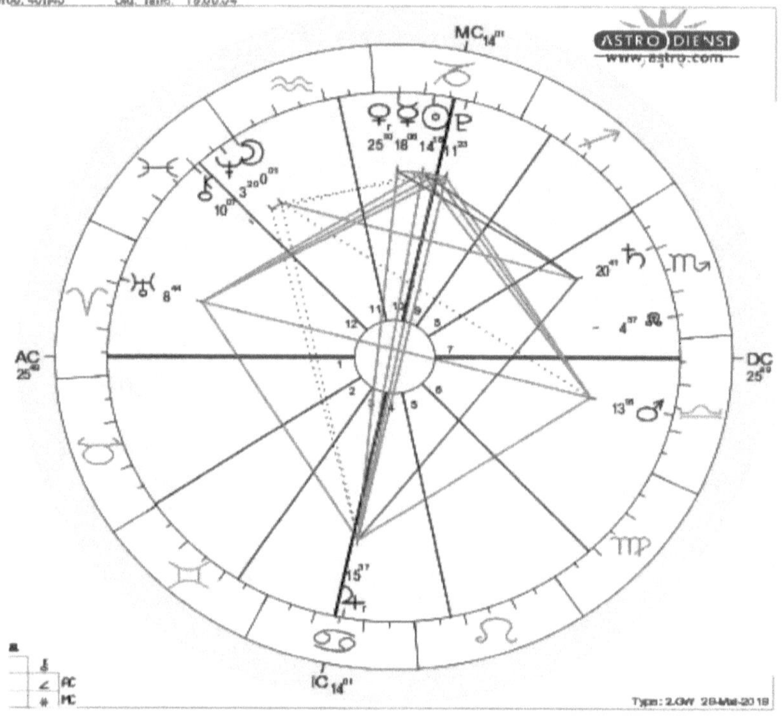

In this chart Jan 4 2014, the degree of mercury(18 degrees) is still higher than the sun's degree(14 degrees), so the **"Figure Set 2"** parameters still apply. When looking at the chart, the last parameter that would have applied from **"Figure Set 2"** would be parameter 9. When the moon was in aquarius and within 1 degree of the degree of mercury and after the moon passed the degree of the sun in an air or fire sign(aquarius is an air sign), the parameter defined the value of BTC/ USD to drop. It was down -1.26% that day.

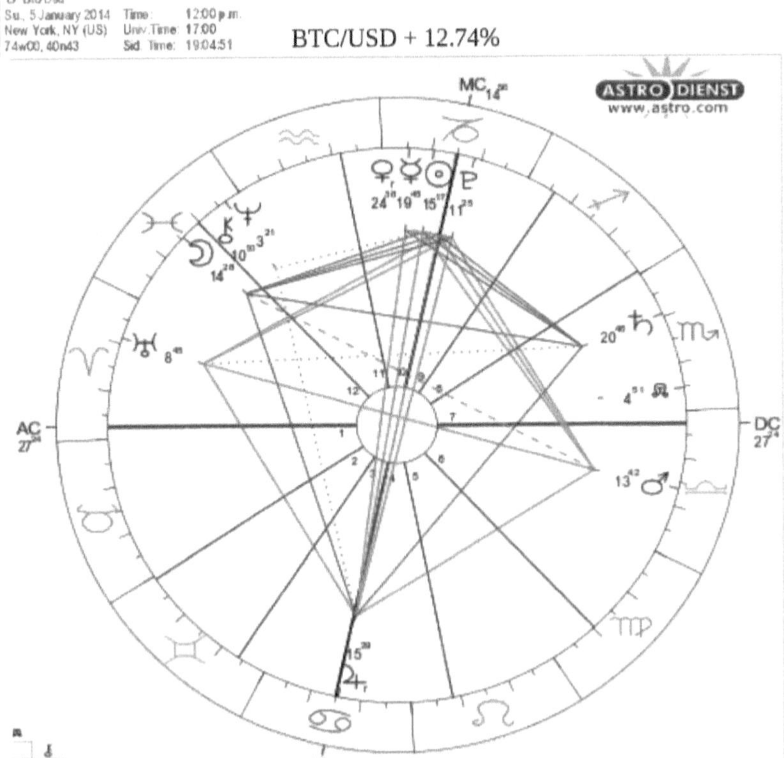

In this chart for Jan 5 2014, the degree of mercury(19 degrees) is still higher than the sun's degree(15 degrees), which means the "**Figure Set 2**" parameters still apply here. When looking at the chart, the last parameter that would have applied from "**Figure Set 2**" would be parameter 6, which says the moon being within 3 degrees of the degree of the sun in an earth or water sign brings the value of BTC/USD up. Pisces is a water sign. So, the parameter's prediction is correct. BTC/USD rose +12.74%.

BTC/USD + 3.38%

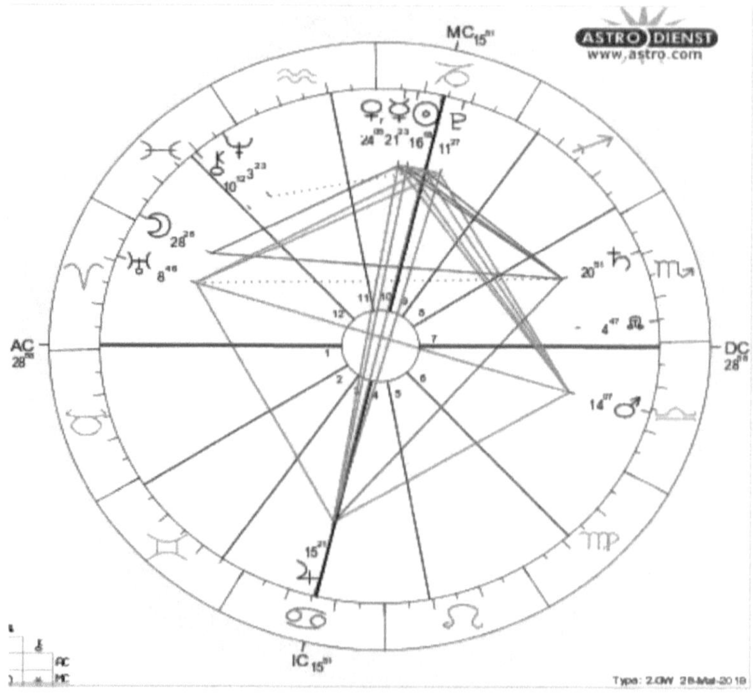

In this chart for Jan 6 2014, the degree of mercury(21 degrees) is still higher than the sun's degree(16 degrees), which means the "**Figure Set 2**" parameters still apply. When looking at the chart, the last parameter that would have applied from "**Figure Set 2**" would be parameter 8, which says the moon being within 1 degree of the degree of the mercury after the moon has passed the degree of the sun in an earth or water sign brings the value of BTC/USD up. Pisces is a water sign. Once again the prediction is correct. BTC/USD rose +3.38% that day.

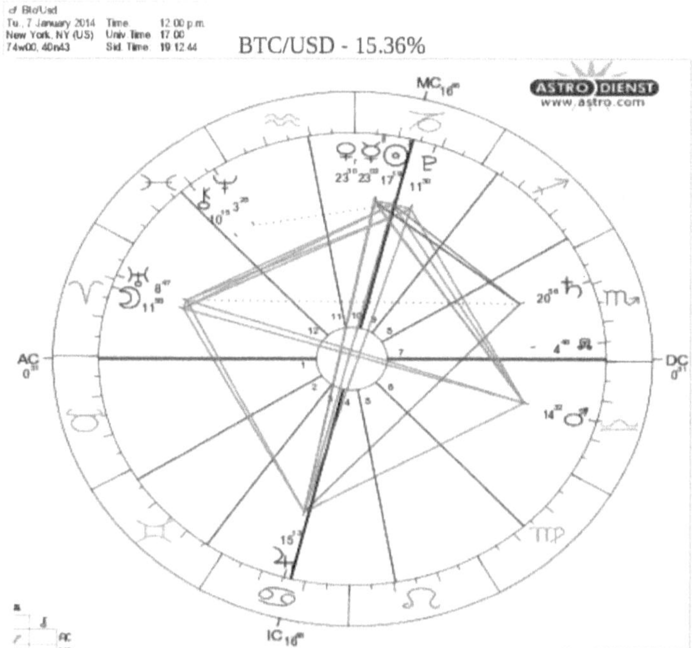

In this chart for Jan 7 2014, the degree of mercury(23 degrees) is still higher than the sun's degree(17 degrees), which means the **"Figure Set 2"** parameters still apply. When looking at the chart, the last parameter that would have applied from **"Figure Set 2"** would be parameter 4, which says the moon being within 1 degree of the degree of the lunar node after the moon passes the degree of the sun in an earth or water sign brings the value of BTC/USD up. The last degree of the sun that was passed by the moon was the 17th degree in pisces, so thus parameter 4 is invoked because Pisces is a water sign. However the prediction from that parameter would be wrong because BTC/USD dropped significantly that day. It was close because Mercury is at 23 degrees. One more degree to 24 degrees and the **"Figure Set 1"** parameters would have been effectuated and the parameter 4 from that set would be correct. Mercury goes into the next sign at 24 degrees which would be counted as a lesser degree than the 17th degree of the sun.

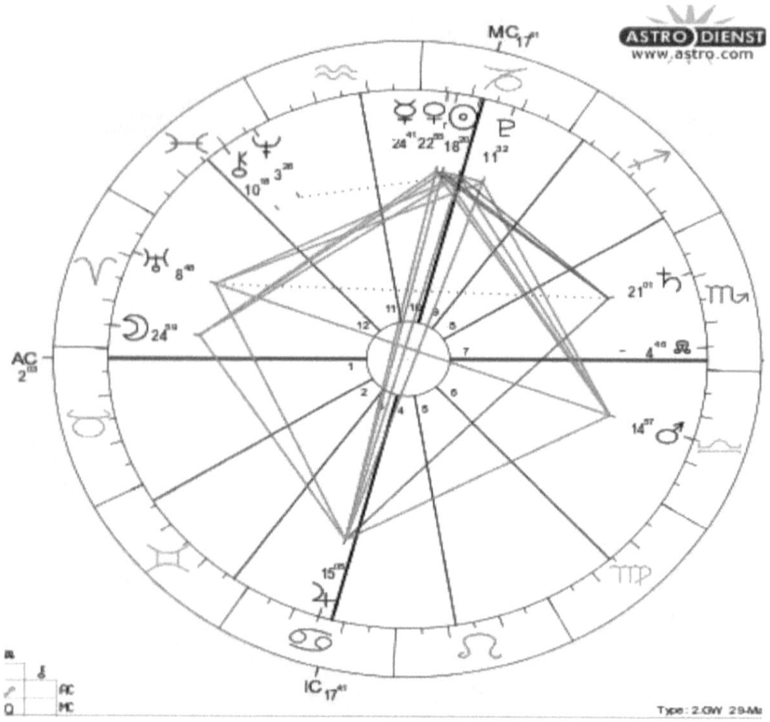

In this chart for Jan 8 2014, the degree of mercury(24 degrees) is lower than the sun's degree(18 degrees). Remember the 24th degree marks the beginning of a new sign. This now means that the **"Figure Set 2"** parameters that we have been using thus far no longer applies at the moment. The **"Figure Set 1"** parameters would now apply. When looking at the chart, the last parameter that would have applied from "Figure Set 1" would be parameter 9, which says the moon being within 1 degree of the degree of mercury after the moon passes the degree of the sun in a fire or air sign brings the value of BTC/ USD up. The last degree being the degree of the sun that was passed by the moon was the 18th degree in Aries before it made its way to within 1 degree of the degree of mercury, so thus parameter 9 is invoked because Aries is a fire sign. The prediction was correct as BTC/ USD rose +4.75% that day.

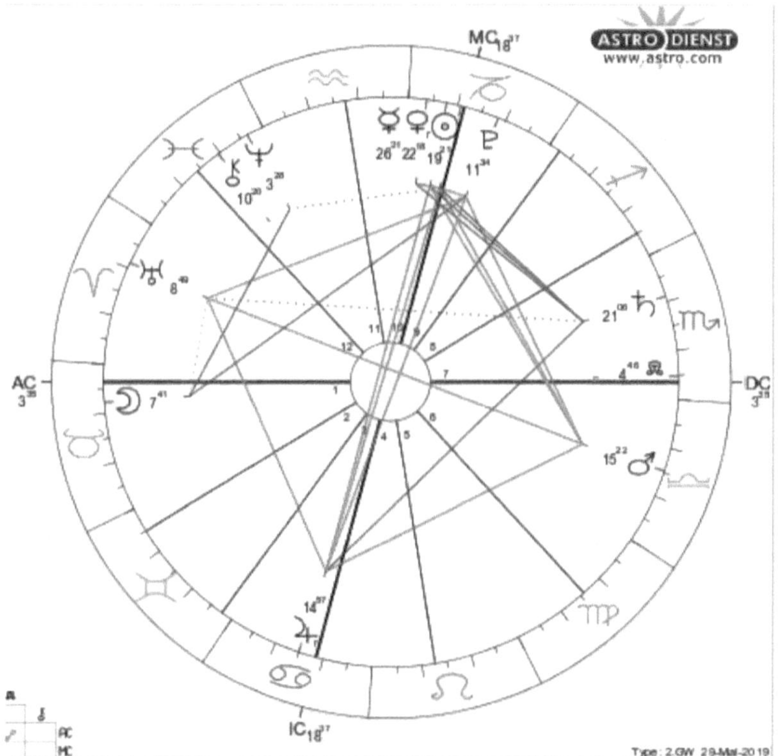

In this chart for Jan 9 2014, the degree of mercury(26 degrees) is lower than the sun's degree(19 degrees). Remember the 24th degree marks the beginning of a new sign. The **"Figure Set 1"** parameters would apply here. When looking at the chart, the last parameter that would have applied from **"Figure Set 1"** would be parameter 5, which says the moon being within 1 degree of the degree of lunar node after the moon passes the degree of the sun in a fire or air sign brings the value of BTC/USD up. The last degree being the degree of the sun that was passed by the moon was the 19th degree in Aries before it made its way to within 1 degree of the degree of lunar node, so thus parameter 5 is invoked because Aries is a fire sign. The prediction was correct as BTC/USD rose +2.59% that day.

BTC/USD -1.79%

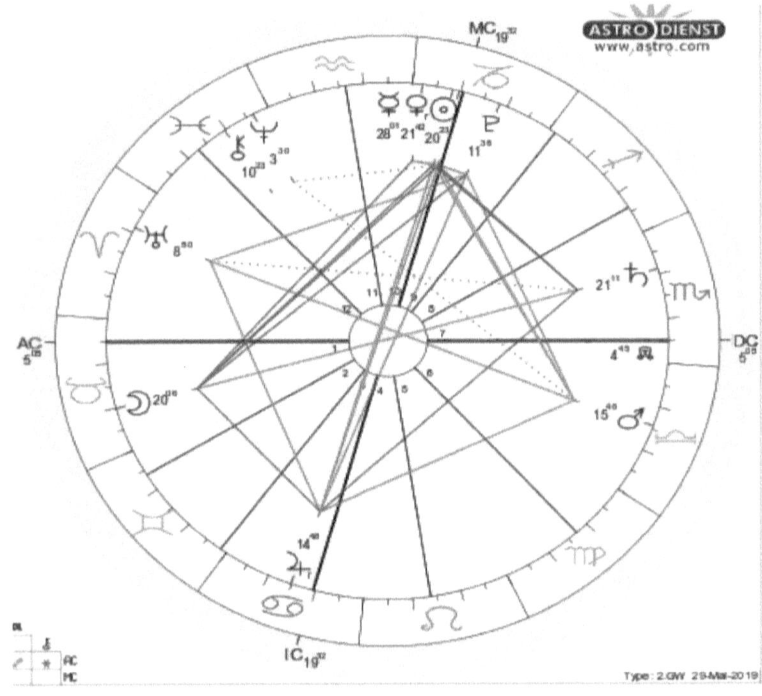

In this chart for Jan 10, 2014, the degree of mercury(28 degrees) is lower than the sun's degree(20 degrees). Remember the 24th degree marks the beginning of a new sign. The **"Figure Set 1"** parameters on would apply here. When looking at the chart, the last parameter that would have applied from **"Figure Set 1"** would be parameter 1, which says the moon being within 1 degree of the degree of the sun in an Earth or water sign brings the value of BTC/USD up. That didn't happen because BTC/USD was down this day. However, it would only be 2 hours before the time used to calculate this chart that parameter 6 would have applied, which states that the moon within 3 degrees of the degree of the sun in an earth or water sin brings the value of BTC/USD down.

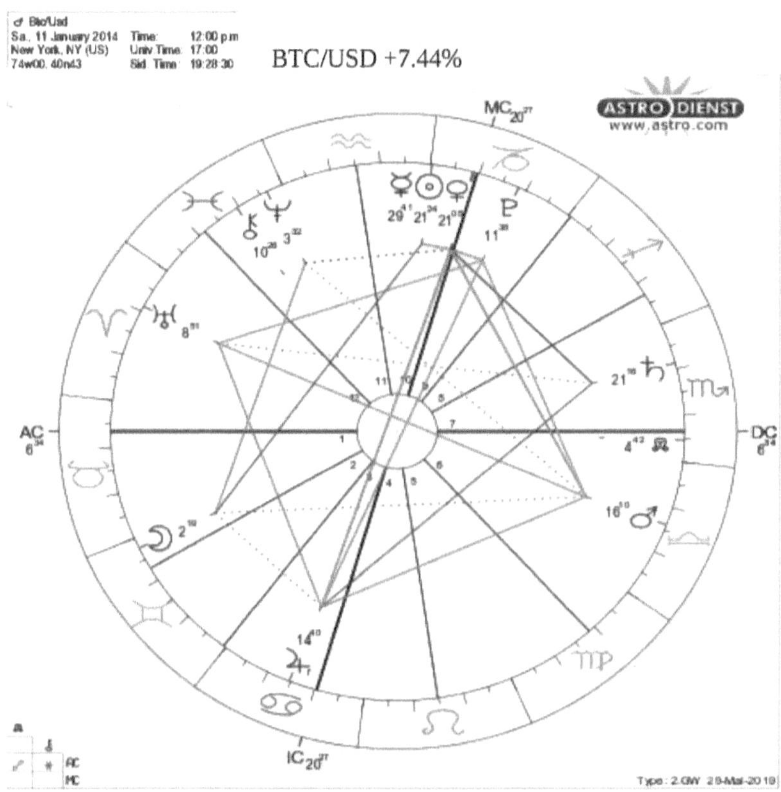

In this chart for Jan 11, 2014, the degree of mercury(29 degrees) is lower than the sun's degree(20 degrees). Remember the 24th degree marks the beginning of a new sign. The **"Figure Set 1"** parameters would apply here. When looking at the chart, the last parameter that would have applied from **"Figure Set 1"** would be parameter 8, which says the moon within 1 degree of the degree of the mercury after the moon has passed the degree of the sun in an Earth or water sign brings the value of BTC/ USD down. That didn't happen because BTC/USD was up significantly this day. So, we have another wrong prediction.

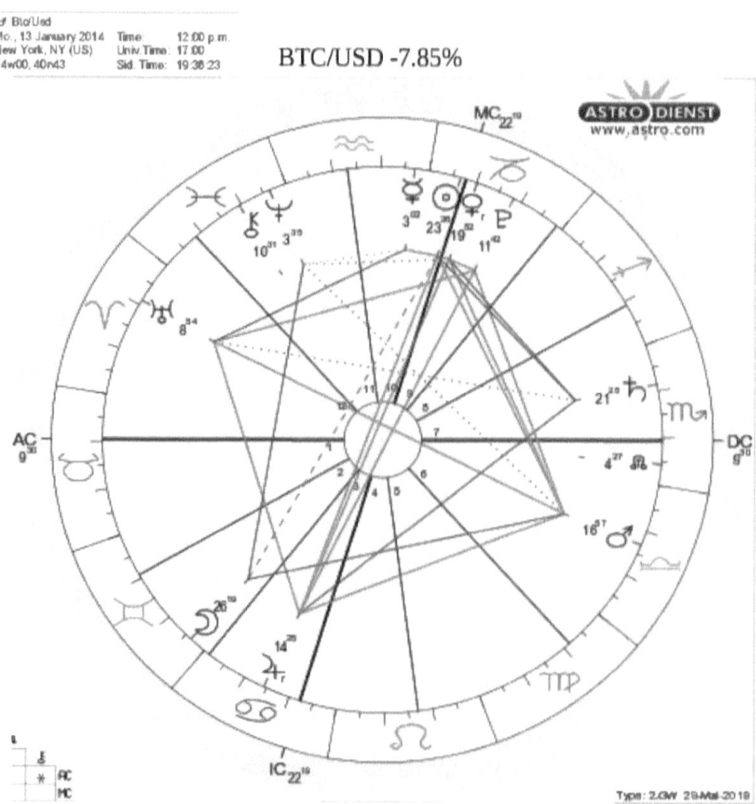

In this chart for Jan 13, 2014, the degree of mercury(3 degrees) is lower than the sun's degree(23 degrees). Remember the 24th degree marks the beginning of a new sign. The "**Figure Set 1**" parameters would apply here. When looking at the chart, the last parameter that would have applied from "**Figure Set 1**" would be parameter 2, which says the moon within 1 degree of the degree of the sun in a Fire or Air sign brings the value of BTC/USD down. The degree of the sun, in this case of the moon going to within 1 degree of the degree of the sun, would be the 23rd degree mark of gemini, which is an air sign. So from that standpoint, the prediction is correct as BTC/USD dropped that day.

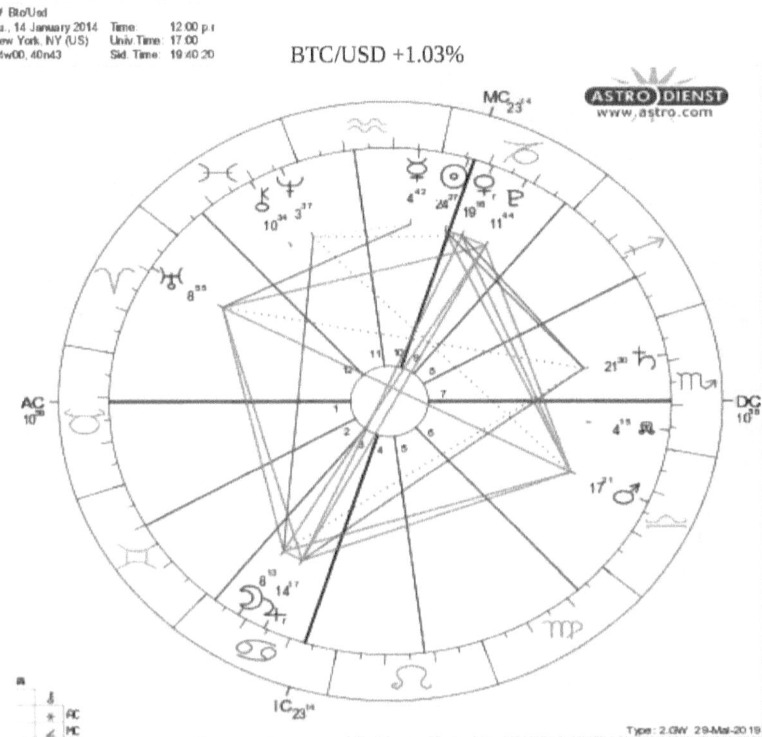

In this chart for Jan 14, 2014, the degree of mercury(4 degrees) is higher than the sun's degree(24 degrees). Remember the 24th degree marks the beginning of a new sign. Therefore, the **"Figure Set 1"** parameters that we have been using no longer apply for now. Because Mercury is at a higher degree than the degree of the sun, we go back to the **"Figure Set 2"** parameters which is invoked when that happens. When looking at the chart, the last parameter that would have applied from **"Figure Set 2"** on would be parameter 8, which says the moon within 1 degree of the degree of the Mercury after the moon has passed the sun's degree in an Earth or water sign brings the value of BTC/USD up. The degree of the sun is 24 degrees, and since the 24th degree marks the beginning of the next sign, the 24th degree mark in gemini is interpreted to the sign of Cancer, which is a water sign. The prediction would be correct as BTC/USD was up 1.03%.

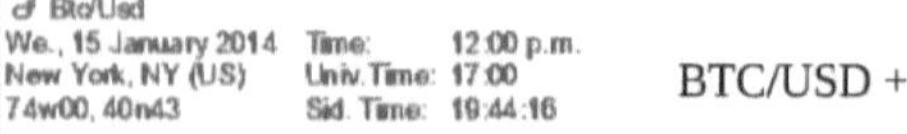

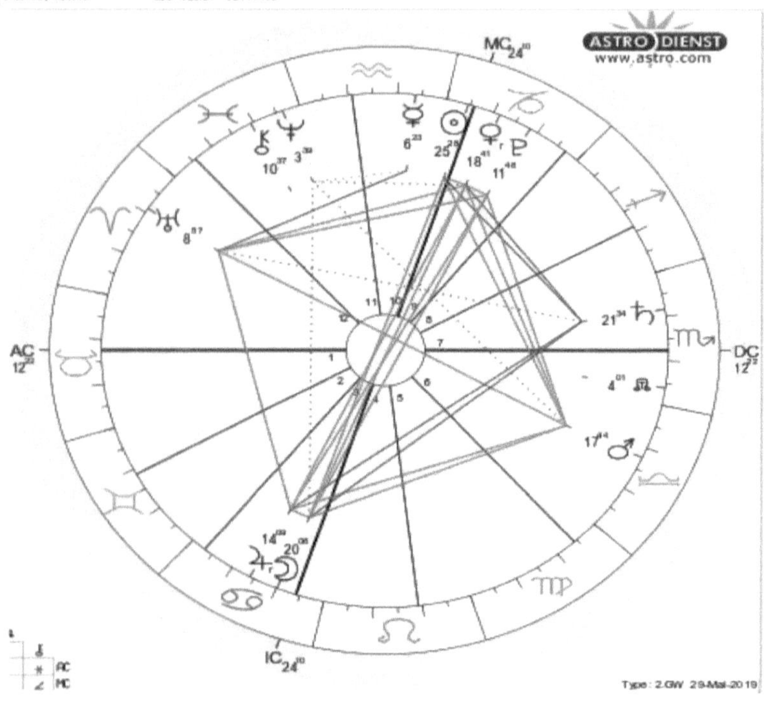

In this chart for Jan 15, 2014, the degree of mercury(6 degrees) is higher than the sun's degree(25 degrees). Remember the 24th degree marks the beginning of a new sign. Because Mercury's degree is at a higher degree than the degree of the sun, we use **"Figure Set 2"** parameters, which is invoked when that happens. When looking at the chart, the last parameter that would have applied from **"Figure Set 2"** would be parameter 8, which says the moon within 1 degree of the degree of Mercury after the moon has passed the sun's degree in an Earth or water sign brings the value of BTC/USD up. That prediction would be correct as BTC/USD was up 1.56% on this day.

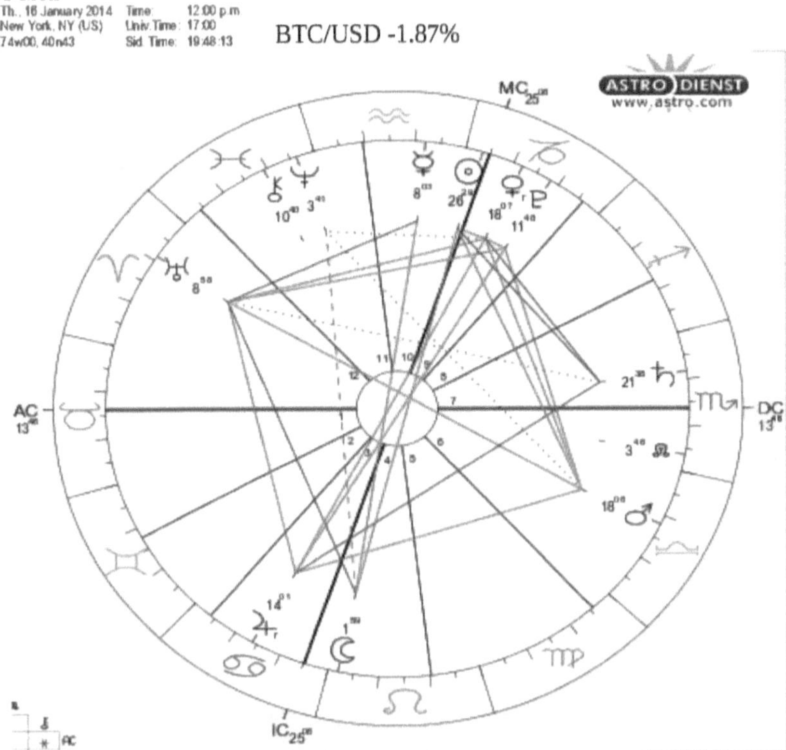

In this chart for Jan 16, 2014, the degree of mercury(8 degrees) is higher than the sun's degree(26 degrees). Remember the 24th degree marks the beginning of a new sign. In light of that, because Mercury's degree is at a higher degree than the degree of the sun, we use **"Figure Set 2"** parameters, which is invoked when that happens. When looking at the chart, the last parameter that would have applied from **"Figure Set 2"** would be parameter 3, which says the moon within 3 degrees of the degree of the Lunar node in any sign brings the value of BTC/USD down. That prediction would be correct as BTC/USD was down -1.87% on this day.

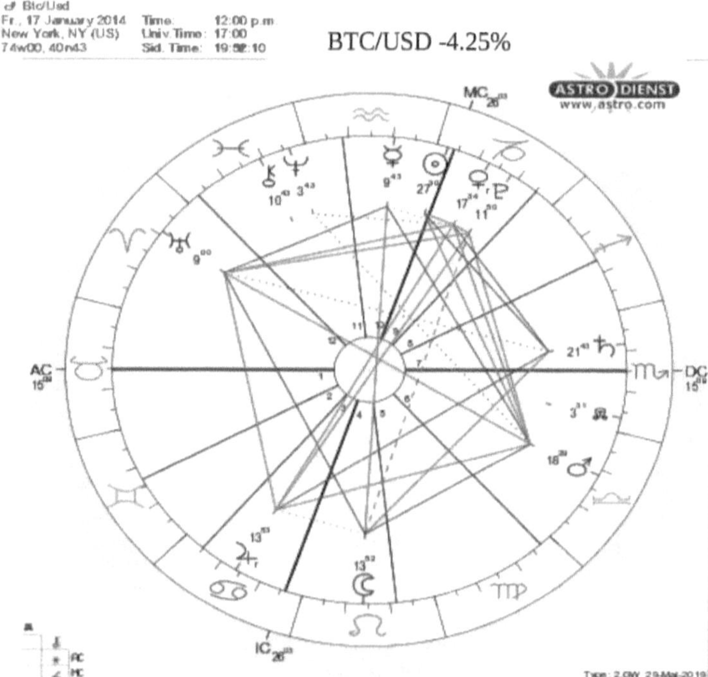

In this chart for Jan 17, 2014, the degree of mercury(9 degrees) is higher than the sun's degree(27 degrees). Remember the 24th degree marks the beginning of a new sign. In light of that, because Mercury's degree is at a higher degree than the degree of the sun, we use **"Figure Set 2"** parameters, which is invoked when that happens. When looking at the chart, the last parameter that would have applied from **"Figure Set 2"** would be parameter 9, which says the moon within 1 degree of the degree of Mercury after the moon has passed the sun's degree in an air or fire sign brings the value of BTC/USD down. The degree of the sun is 27 degrees, and that 27th degree mark for this parameter applied at the 27 degree mark of Cancer, which is interpreted to Leo because the 24th degree mark marks the beginning of the next sign, which in this case is Leo, which is also a fire sign. In that regard, parameter 9 is applied and the prediction would be correct as BTC/USD was down -4.25% on this day.

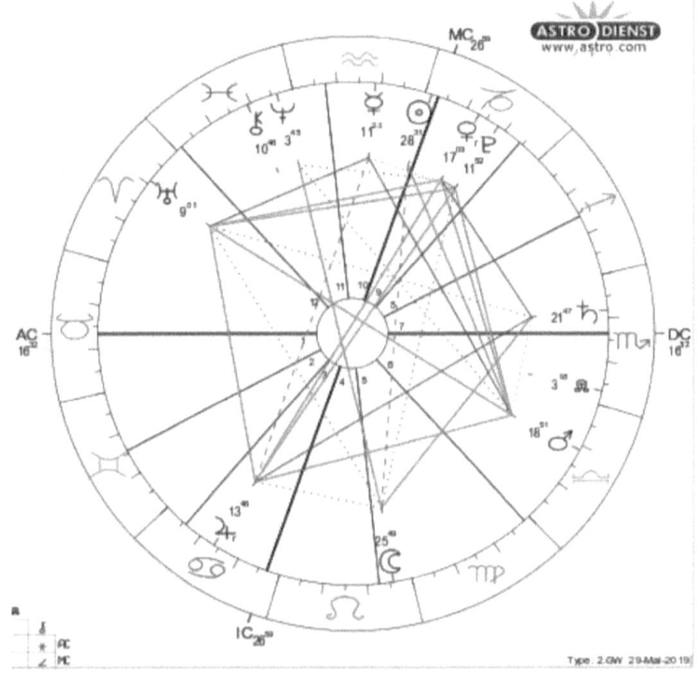

In this chart for Jan 18, 2014, the degree of mercury(11 degrees) is higher than the sun's degree(28 degrees). Remember, the 24th degree marks the beginning of a new sign. So therefore, 11 degrees is later in the sign than 28 degrees, which thus makes the 11th degree higher than the 28th degree. In light of that, because Mercury's degree is at a higher degree than the degree of the sun, we use **"Figure Set 2"** parameters, which is invoked when that happens. When looking at the chart, the last parameter that would have applied from **"Figure Set 2"** would be parameter 6, which says the moon within 3 degrees of the degree of the sun in an earth or water sign brings the value of BTC/USD up. The moon at 25 degrees is 3 degrees from the 28 degree mark of Leo which is the degree of the sun. That 28th degree mark is interpreted to the next sign of Virgo, which is an Earth sign and thus a fulfilled requirement for parameter 6. This prediction would be correct as BTC/USD was up +1.39% for this day.

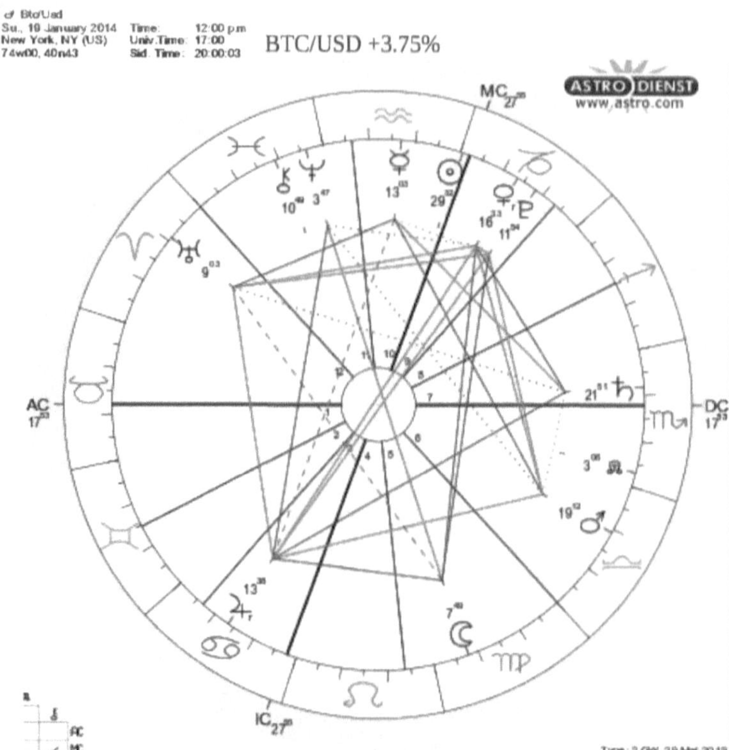

In this chart for Jan 19, 2014, the degree of mercury(13 degrees) is higher than the sun's degree(29 degrees). Remember, the 24th degree marks the beginning of a new sign. Therefore, the 13th degree would be considered higher than the 29th degree. In light of that, because Mercury's degree is at a higher degree than the degree of the sun, we use **"Figure Set 2"** parameters. When looking at the chart, the last parameter that would have applied from **"Figure Set 2"** would be parameter 4, which says the moon within 1 degree of the degree of the lunar node after the moon has passed the sun's degree in an earth of water sign brings the value of BTC/USD up. Because the sun is 29 degrees, the degree of sun for this parameter would have applied to the 29th degree of Leo, which is thus interpreted to the sign of Virgo, which is an earth sign. This prediction would be correct as BTC/USD was up +3.75% for this day.

We will skip to Jan 24, 2014 since that's the next significant price change

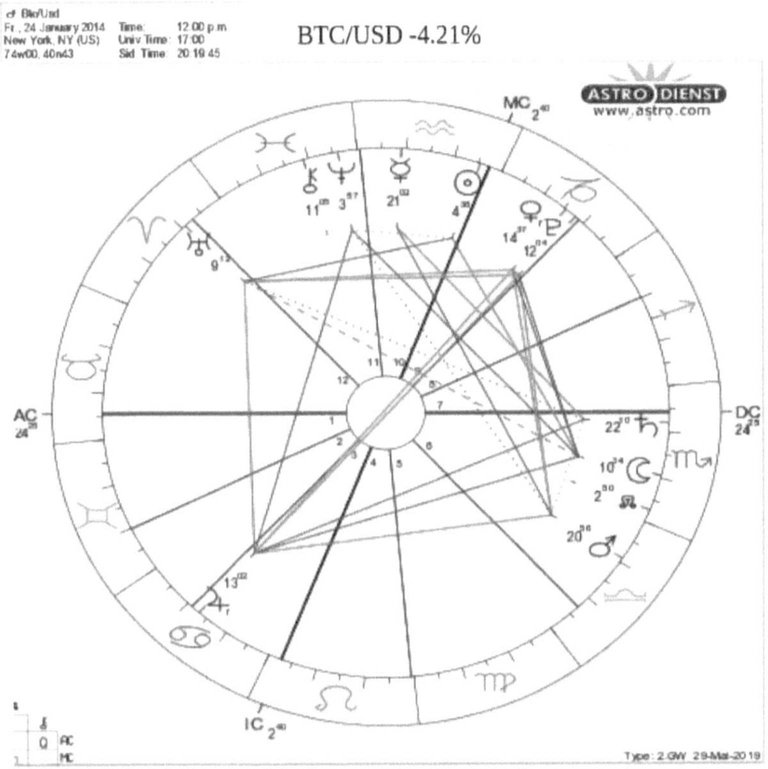

In this chart for Jan 24, 2014, the degree of mercury(21 degrees) is higher than the sun's degree(4 degrees). Therefore, we continue to use **"Figure Set 2"** parameters. When looking at the chart, the last parameter that would have applied from **"Figure Set 2"** would be parameter 1, which says the moon within 1 degree of the degree of the sun in an earth or water sign brings the value of BTC/USD down. Since the Sun is at 4 degrees, the degree of the sun referred to in this case is the 4th degree of Scorpio, which is a water sign. The prediction would be correct as BTC/USD was down -4.21% for this day.

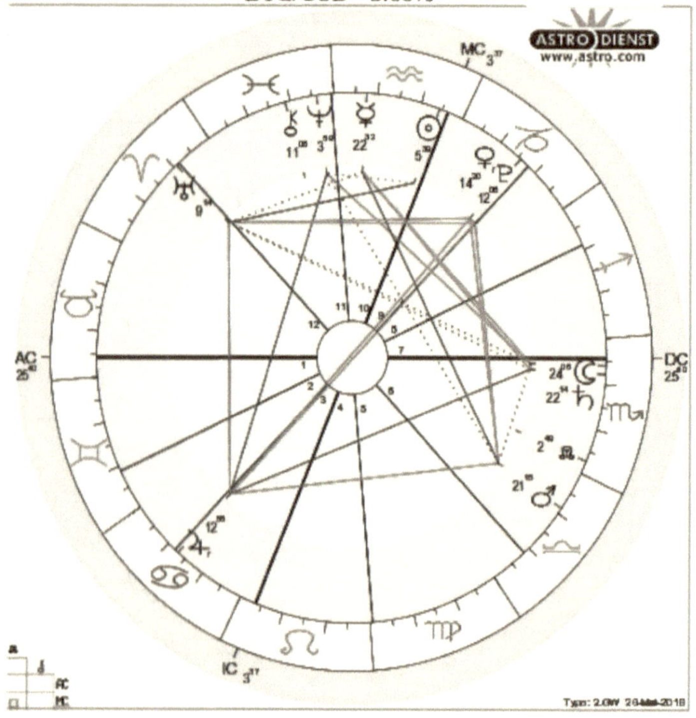

In this chart for Jan 25, 2014, the degree of mercury(22 degrees) is higher than the sun's degree(5 degrees). Therefore, we continue to use **"Figure Set 2"** parameters. When looking at the chart, the last parameter that would have applied from **"Figure Set 2"** would be parameter 8, which says the moon within 1 degree of the degree of mercury after the moon has passed the sun's degree in an earth or water sign brings the value of BTC/USD up. Since the Sun is at 5 degrees, the degree of the sun referred to in this case is the 5th degree of Scorpio, which is a water sign. This prediction would be correct as BTC/USD was up +3.60% for this day.

We will skip to Jan 27, 2014 since that's the next significant price change

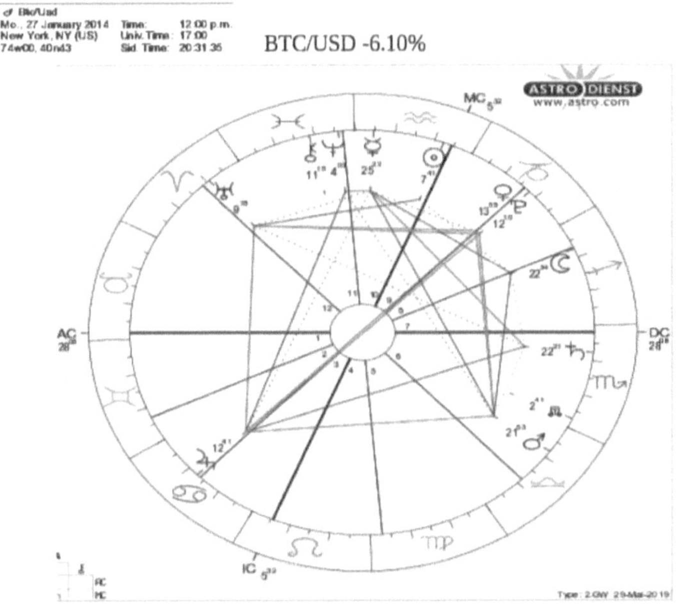

In this chart for Jan 27, 2014, Mercury enters a new sign. Since the 24th degree marks the start of a new sign and Mercury is at 25 degrees in this chart, its now observed for the degree of the mercury to be lower than the degree of the sun. In this case, mercury's degree(25 degrees) is lower than the degree of the sun(7 degrees). Therefore, we stop using the **"Figure Set 2"** parameters and start back again with the **"Figure Set 1"** parameters. These are applied when the degree of mercury is lower than the degree of the sun. When looking at the chart, the last parameter that would have applied from **"Figure Set 1"** would be parameter 2, which says the moon within 1 degree of the degree of the sun in a fire or air sign brings the value of BTC/USD down. Since the Sun is at 7 degrees, the degree of the sun referred to in this case of the moon within 1 degree is the 7th degree mark of Sagittarius, which is a fire sign. Therefore, this prediction would be correct as BTC/USD was down -6.10% for this day.

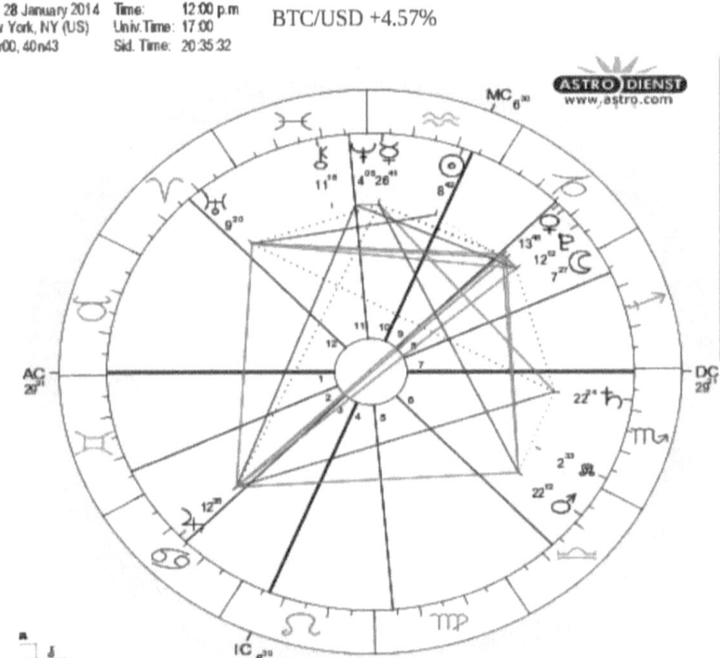

In this chart for Jan 28, 2014, mercury's degree(26 degrees) is lower than the degree of the sun(8 degrees) . Therefore, we use the "**Figure Set 1**" parameters. These are applied when the degree of mercury is lower than the degree of the sun. When looking at the chart, the last parameter that would have applied from **"Figure Set 1"** would be parameter 1, which says the moon within 1 degree of the degree of the sun in an earth or water sign brings the value of BTC/USD up. In this chart, the moon is not exact to within 1 degree of the degree of the sun at 12pm ....so technically in doesn't apply in the way that I was counting it in previous examples---having to be within the exact 1 degree mark down to the superscript(the small number above the number). But since within 1 hour from the time used to calculate the chart, the 1ˢᵗ parameter would eventually end up applying, we use it in this case anyway. Therefore, we can say this prediction would be correct as BTC/ USD was up +4.57% for this day.

We'll end the January there and move onto February to see if the parameters will continue to correlate with the value of BTC/USD. Below are the prices for BTC/USD during the month of February 2014. We will continue with the same algorithm

Date	Price	Open	High	Low	Vol.	Change %	
Feb 28, 2014	565.0	575.5	590.3	544.9	0.34K	-2.42%	
Feb 27, 2014	579.0	592.5	592.5	565.7	0.01K	-0.52%	These are the
Feb 26, 2014	582.0	548.7	594.5	544.0	0.72K	13.01%	prices for the
Feb 25, 2014	515.0	554.0	567.0	425.0	1.91K	-8.43%	BTC/USD for
Feb 24, 2014	562.4	597.3	597.3	562.4	0.01K	-9.14%	the month of
Feb 23, 2014	619.0	597.7	624.1	597.7	0.02K	4.00%	February
Feb 22, 2014	595.2	587.6	602.8	563.7	0.00K	4.79%	2014
Feb 21, 2014	568.0	565.2	591.5	548.5	0.06K	-1.88%	
Feb 20, 2014	578.9	633.0	633.0	574.8	0.04K	-8.17%	
Feb 19, 2014	630.4	634.2	638.0	628.0	0.10K	0.38%	
Feb 18, 2014	628.0	660.0	660.0	622.0	0.05K	-5.40%	
Feb 17, 2014	663.8	626.0	663.8	626.0	0.03K	9.19%	
Feb 16, 2014	608.0	650.0	650.0	608.0	0.11K	-6.95%	
Feb 15, 2014	653.4	652.9	655.7	650.0	0.02K	-4.20%	
Feb 14, 2014	682.0	622.0	724.0	565.2	0.46K	7.53%	
Feb 13, 2014	634.3	671.9	671.9	630.0	0.04K	-7.41%	
Feb 12, 2014	685.0	691.1	691.1	650.0	0.06K	3.97%	
Feb 11, 2014	658.9	739.0	761.7	653.3	0.13K	-6.72%	
Feb 10, 2014	706.3	720.0	739.0	642.0	0.11K	-0.52%	
Feb 09, 2014	710.0	702.6	720.0	702.6	0.10K	2.90%	
Feb 08, 2014	690.0	700.0	716.4	690.0	0.05K	-4.17%	
Feb 07, 2014	720.0	750.3	755.1	677.0	0.28K	-6.68%	
Feb 06, 2014	771.6	793.0	793.0	768.0	0.16K	-2.46%	
Feb 05, 2014	791.0	807.0	808.0	791.0	0.33K	-2.71%	
Feb 04, 2014	813.0	810.8	813.2	808.3	0.12K	0.37%	
Feb 03, 2014	810.0	806.8	814.1	801.7	0.14K	-0.57%	
Feb 01, 2014	814.6	801.9	814.6	801.9	0.01K	1.83%	

Highest: 814.6 Lowest: 425.0 Difference: 389.6 Average: 660.5

Change %: -29.4

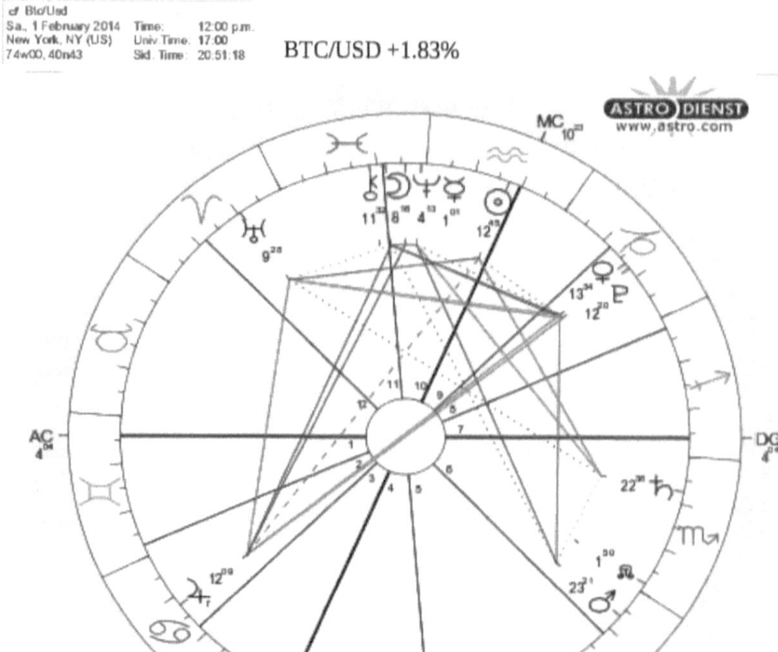

In this chart for Feb 1, 2014, mercury's degree(1 degree) is lower than the degree of the sun(12 degrees). Therefore, we continue to use the "**Figure Set 1**" parameters. These are applied when the degree of mercury is lower than the degree of the sun. When looking at the chart, the last parameter that would have applied from "**Figure Set 1**" would be parameter 9, which says the moon within 1 degree of the degree of mercury after the moon has passed the sun's degree in an air or fire sign brings the value of BTC/ USD up. The last degree of the sun that the moon passed was the 12th degree in Aquarius, which is an air sign. Therefore this prediction is accurate. BTC/USD was up +1.83%.

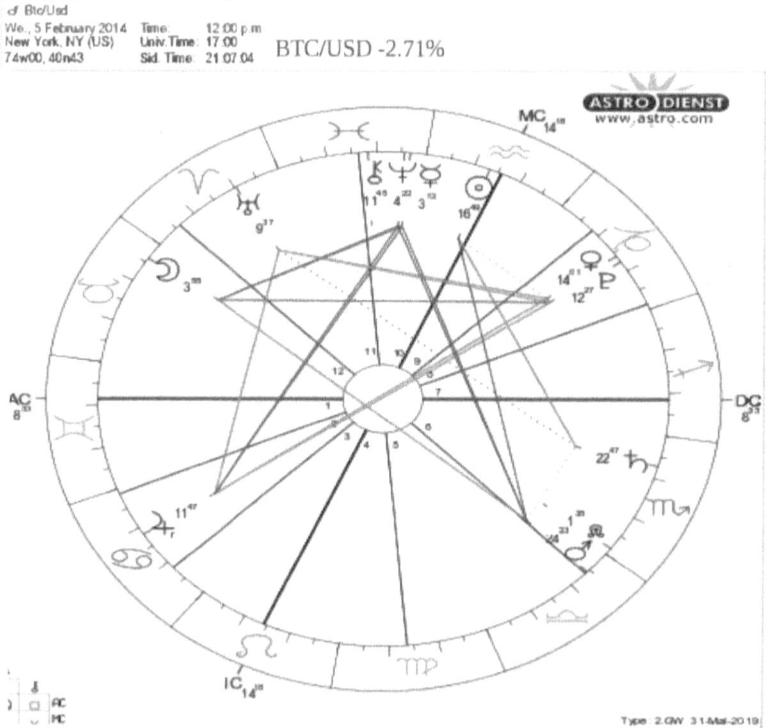

In this chart for Feb 5, 2014, mercury's degree(3 degrees) is still lower than the degree of the sun(16 degrees). Therefore, we continue to use the **"Figure Set 1"** parameters. When looking at the chart, the last parameter that would have applied from **"Figure Set 1"** would be parameter 9, which says the moon within 1 degree of the degree of mercury after the moon has passed the sun's degree in an air or fire sign brings the value of BTC/ USD up. The last degree of the sun that the moon passed was the 12th degree in Aries, which is fire sign. Therefore this prediction is wrong. BTC/USD was actually down -2.71%.

note: there will be days when the parameters will be wrong.

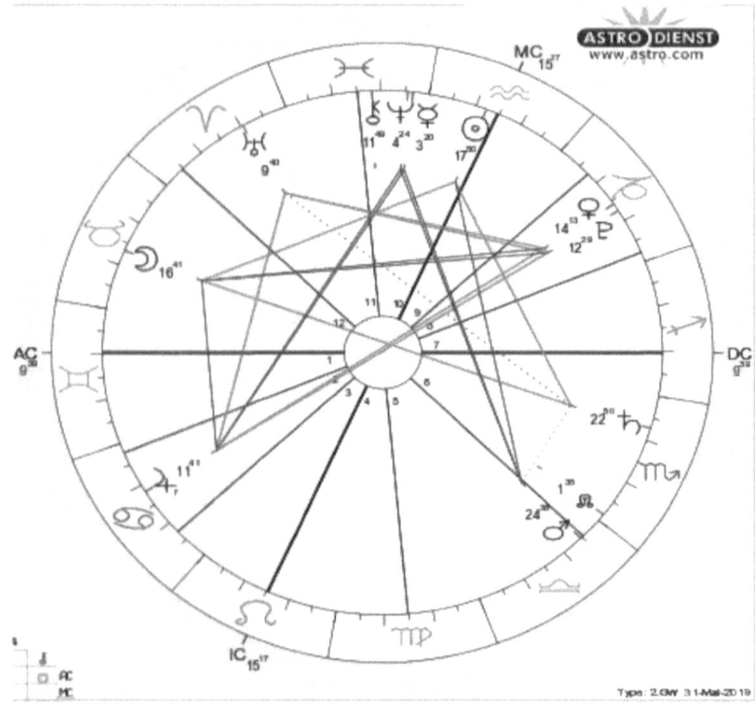

In this chart for Feb 6, 2014, mercury's degree(3 degrees) is lower than the degree of the sun(17 degrees). Therefore, we continue to use the **"Figure Set 1"** parameters. When looking at the chart, the last parameter that would have applied from **"Figure Set 1"** would be parameter 6, which says the moon within 3 degrees of the degree of the sun in an earth or water sign brings the value of BTC/USD down. This prediction is correct. BTC/USD was down -2.46%.

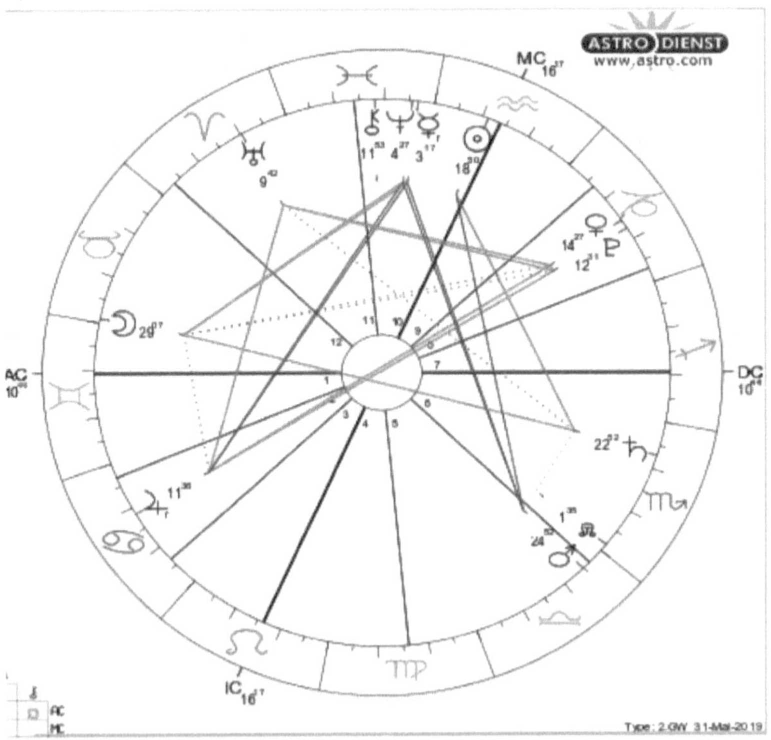

In this chart for Feb 7, 2014, mercury's degree(3 degrees) is lower than the degree of the sun(18 degrees). Therefore, we continue to use the **"Figure Set 1"** parameters. When looking at the chart, the last parameter that would have applied from **"Figure Set 1"** would be parameter 3, which says the moon within 3 degrees of the degree of the lunar node in any sign brings the value of BTC/USD down. The lunar node is at 1 degree and the moon is at 29 degrees. So this applies because the moon is 2 degrees away from the lunar node, which is within the determined 3 degrees to effectuate the prediction. This prediction is correct. BTC/USD was down -6.68%.

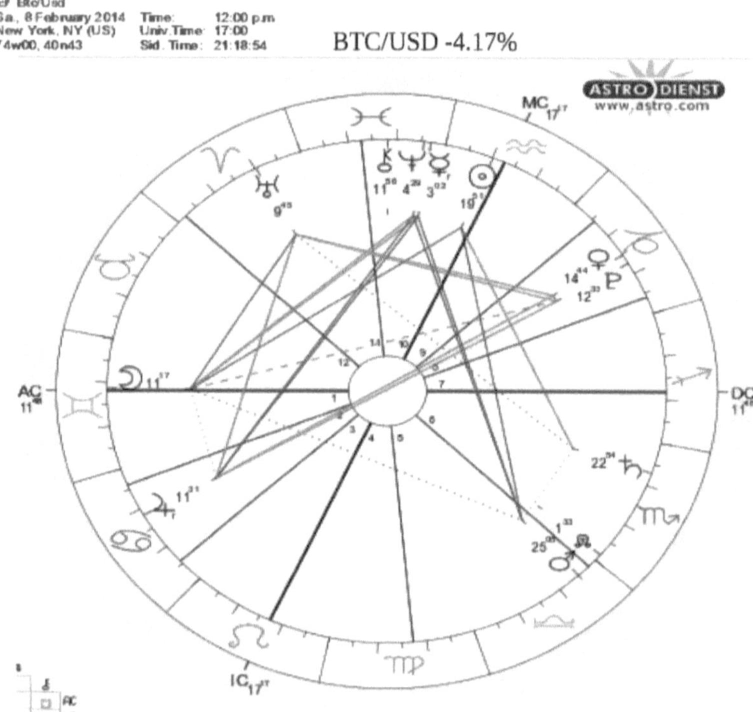

In this chart for Feb 8, 2014, mercury's degree(3 degrees) is lower than the degree of the sun(19 degrees). Therefore, we continue to use the **"Figure Set 1"** parameters. When looking at the chart, the last parameter that would have applied from **"Figure Set 1"** would be parameter 8, which says the moon within 1 degree of the degree of mercury after the moon has passed the sun's degree in an Earth or Water sign brings the value of BTC/USD down. The degree of the sun is 19, and the last degree of the sun passed by the moon in this chart was the 19th degree in Taurus, which is an earth sign. Therefore, this prediction is correct. BTC/USD was down -4.17%.

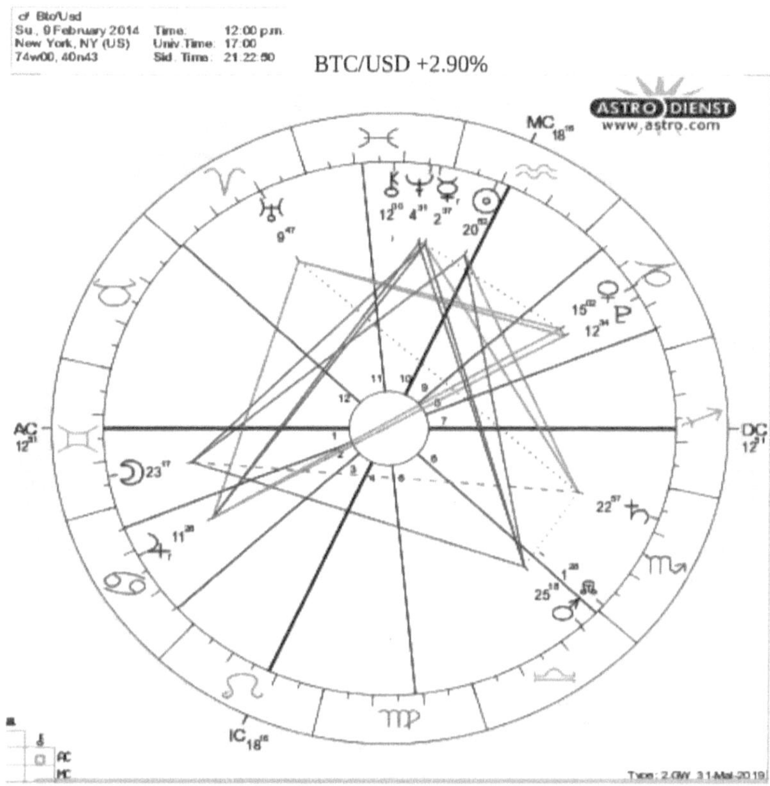

In this chart for Feb 9, 2014, mercury's degree(2 degrees) is lower than the degree of the sun(20 degrees). Therefore, we continue to use the **"Figure Set 1"** parameters. When looking at the chart, the last parameter that would have applied from **"Figure Set 1"** would be parameter 2, which says the moon within 1 degree of the degree of the sun in an Air or Fire sign brings the value of BTC/USD down. Gemini is an air sign Therefore, this prediction is WRONG. BTC/USD was up +2.90% this day. .

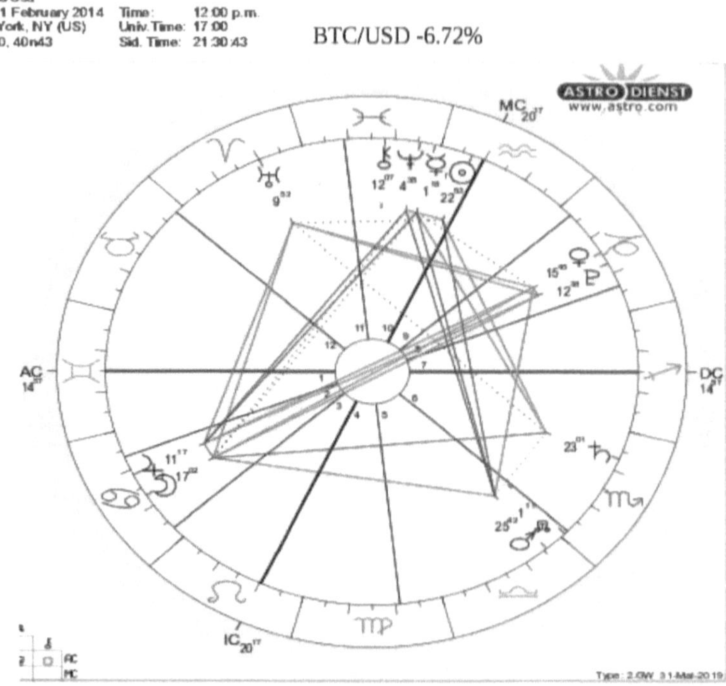

In this chart for Feb 11, 2014, mercury's degree(1 degree) is lower than the degree of the sun(22 degrees). Therefore, we continue to use the **"Figure Set 1"** parameters. When looking at the chart, the last parameter that would have applied from **"Figure Set 1"** would be parameter 9, which says the moon within 1 degree of the degree of mercury after the moon has passed the sun's degree in an Air or Fire sign brings the value of BTC/USD up. That last sun's degree of 22 was passed by the moon in Gemini which is an air sign. Therefore, this prediction is WRONG. BTC/ USD was down -6.72% this day. This could only be resolved by the fact that the moon would have been within 3 degrees of the degree of the sun in about 4 hours from the time used to calculate the chart. That would have invoked a prediction for BTC/USD to drop.

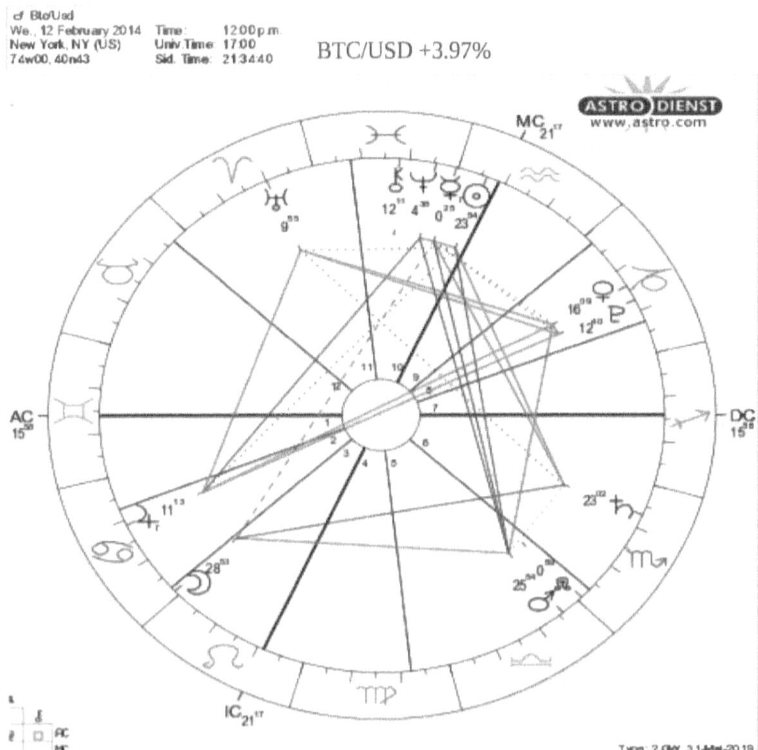

In this chart for Feb 12, 2014, mercury's degree(0 degree) is lower than the degree of the sun(23 degrees). Therefore, we continue to use the "**Figure Set 1**" parameters. When looking at the chart, the last parameter that would have applied from "**Figure Set 1**" would be parameter 3, which says the moon within 3 degrees of the degree of the lunar node in any sign brings the value of BTC/USD down. With the moon at 28 degrees and the lunar node at 0 degrees, we see that the parameter is taking place, however the prediction is wrong again. BTC/USD rose +3.97%. However in about 3 hours from the time used to calculate the chart, the sun would have went into the next sign and the moon would have traveled about 2 degrees. This would invoke another set and another parameter which would predict the BTC/USD to rise.

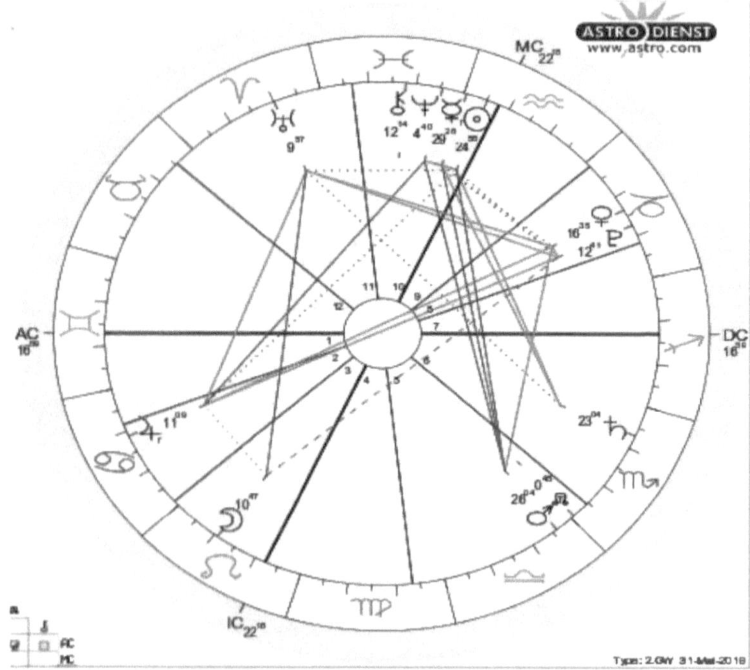

In this chart for Feb 13, 2014, the Sun enters a new sign at the 24 degree mark. This means that mercury's degree(29 degrees) is now higher than the degree of the sun(24 degrees). Therefore, we stop using the "**Figure Set 1**" parameters and start using the "**Figure Set 2**" parameters again. "**Figure Set 2**" parameters are applied when the degree of mercury is higher than the degree of the sun. When looking at the chart, the last parameter that would have applied from "**Figure Set 2**" would be parameter 5, which says the moon within 1 degree of the degree of the lunar node after the moon has passed the sun's degree in an air or fire sign brings the value of BTC/USD down. The 24th degree, which is the degree of the sun in this chart and also the beginning of the next sign, would have been passed by the moon at the 24th degree of Cancer, which is interpreted to Leo, which is a fire sign. Therefore the prediction is correct. BTC/USD was down -7.41%.

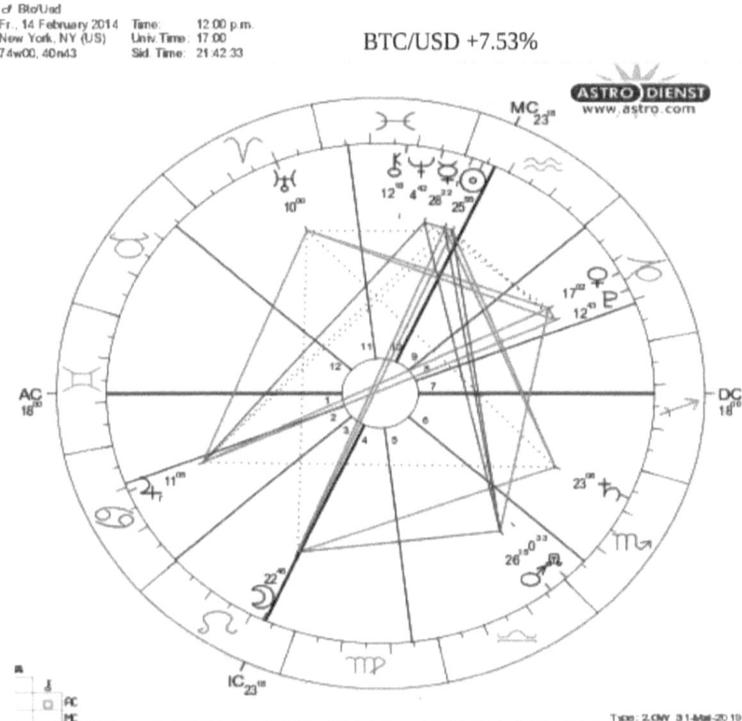

In this chart for Feb 14, 2014, mercury's degree(28 degrees) is higher than the sun's degree (25 degrees). Therefore, we use the "**Figure Set 2**" parameters again. "**Figure Set 2**" parameters are applied when the degree of mercury is higher than the degree of the sun. When looking at the chart, the last parameter that would have applied from "**Figure Set 2**" would be parameter 6, which says the moon within 3 degrees of the degree of the sun in an earth or water sign brings the value of BTC/USD up. The degree of the moon is 22 degrees and the degree of the sun is 25 degrees in Aquarius interpreted to Pisces, which is a water sign. That's within 3 degrees of a water sign as defined by the parameter and therefore results in the correct prediction. BTC/USD was up +7.53%.

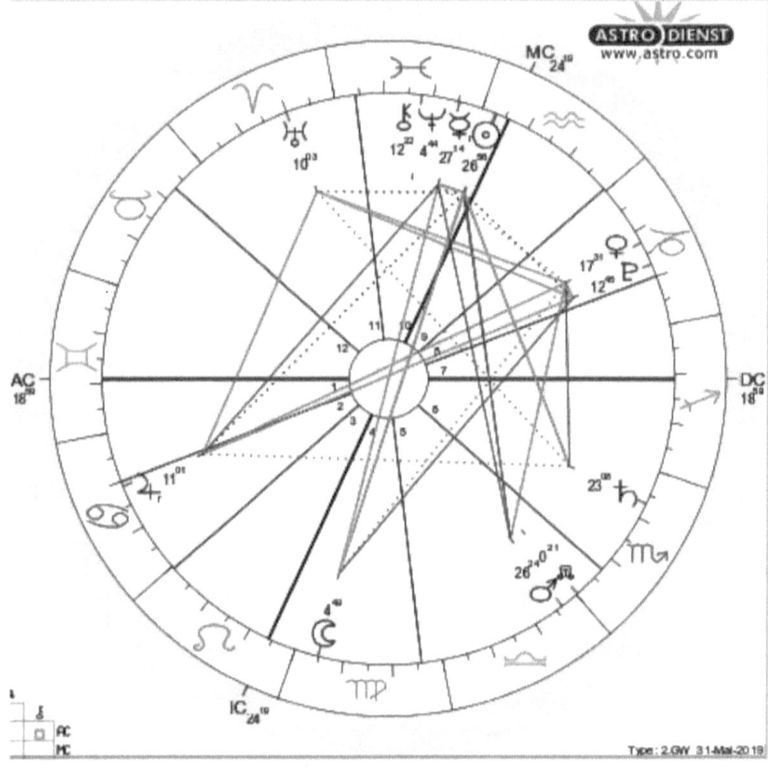

In this chart for Feb 15, 2014, mercury's degree(27 degrees) is higher than the sun's degree (26 degrees). Therefore, we use the **"Figure Set 2"** parameters again. When looking at the chart, the last parameter that would have applied from **"Figure Set 2"** would be parameter 4, which says the moon within 1 degree of the degree of the lunar node after the moon has passed the degree of the sun in an earth or water sign brings the value of BTC/USD up. So this prediction turns out incorrect as BTC/USD was down -4.20%. This can be resolved by looking at the fact that mercury, which is in retrograde, would switch positions with the sun that day by going to a lesser degree than the sun and thus invoking **"Figure Set 1"** parameters, which would give the correct prediction.

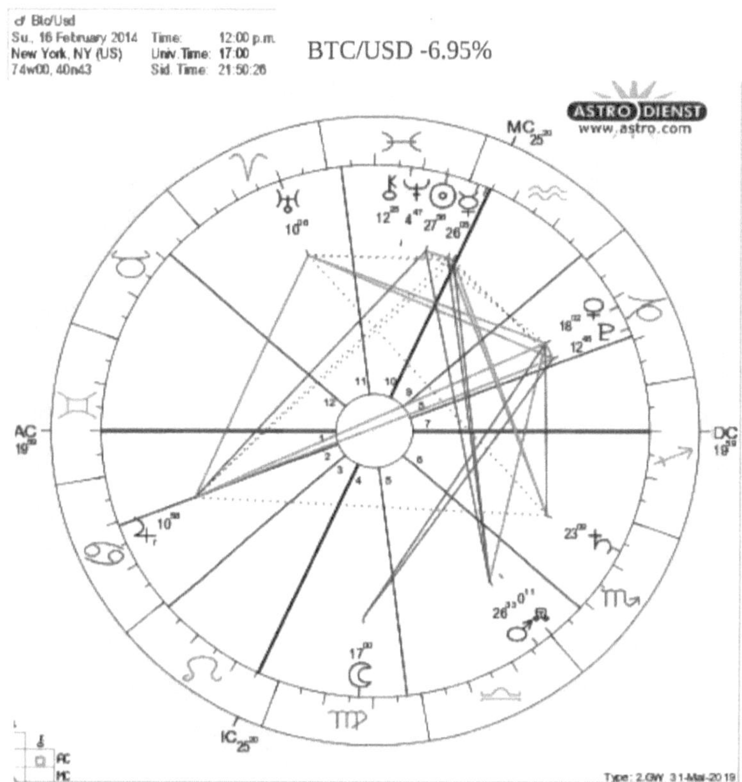

In this chart for Feb 16, 2014, mercury's degree (26 degrees) becomes lower than the sun's degree(27 degrees). Therefore, **"Figure Set 2"** parameters no longer apply here. We now go back to **"Figure Set 1"** parameters. The last parameter from **"Figure Set 1"** that applied in this chart was parameter 4, which says the moon being within 1 degree of the degree of the lunar node after the moon has passed the degree of the sun in an earth or water sign brings the value of BTC/USD down. That occurred here and thus the prediction is correct. BTC/USD was down – 6.95%.

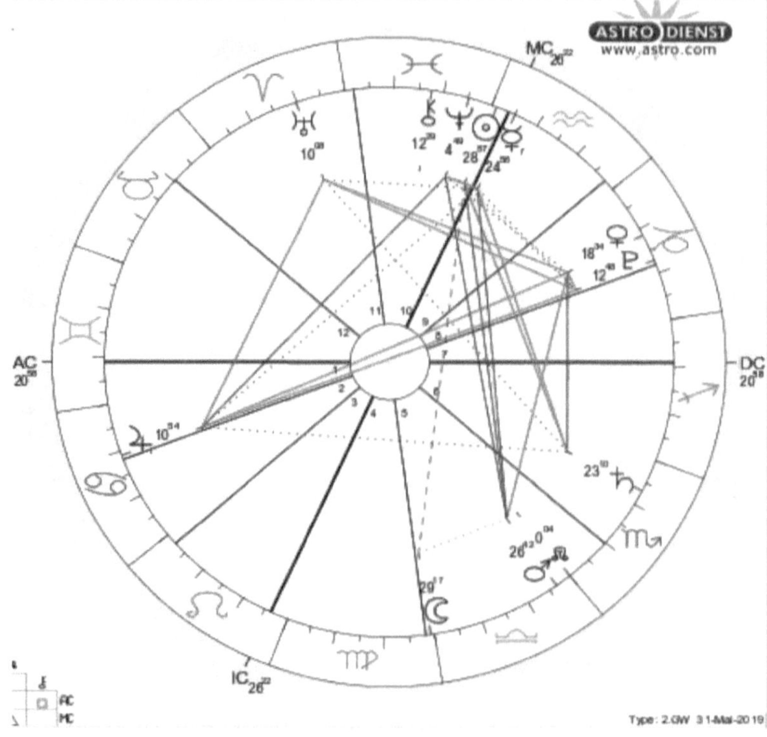

In this chart for Feb 17, 2014, mercury's degree (24 degrees) is lower than the sun's degree(28 degrees). Therefore, **"Figure Set 1"** parameters still apply. The last parameter from **"Figure Set 1"** that applied in this chart was parameter 5, which says the moon being within 1 degree of the degree of the lunar node after the moon has passed the degree of the sun in a fire or air sign brings the value of BTC/USD up. The degree of the moon is at 29 and the degree of the lunar node is at 0. That's within the 1 degree mark stated in the parameter 5 along with the moon having already passed the sun's degree in an air or fire sign as libra is an air sign. This leaves us with another correct prediction. BTC/USD was up +9.19%.

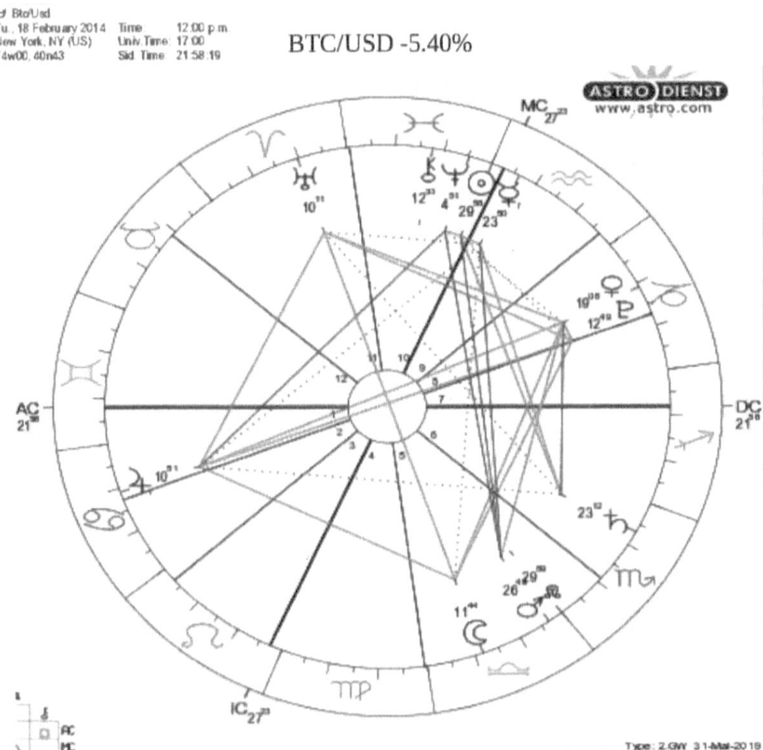

In this chart for Feb 18, 2014, another change in the relationship between the sun and mercury has taken place. Mercury has gone back wards into another sign at the 23rd degree mark. This puts mercury's degree(23 degrees) higher than the sun's degree(29 degrees). (Remember, the 24th degree marks the beginning of a new sign so that makes the 24th degree the lowest numbered degree.) Therefore, **"Figure Set 1"** parameters no longer apply. We go back to **"Figure Set 2"** parameters. The last parameter from **"Figure Set 2"** that would have applied here would be parameter 5, which says the moon being within 1 degree of the degree of the lunar node after the moon has passed the degree of the sun in an air of fire sign bring the value of BTC/USD down. Since Libra is an air sign, this prediction is correct. BTC/USD was down -5.40% this day.

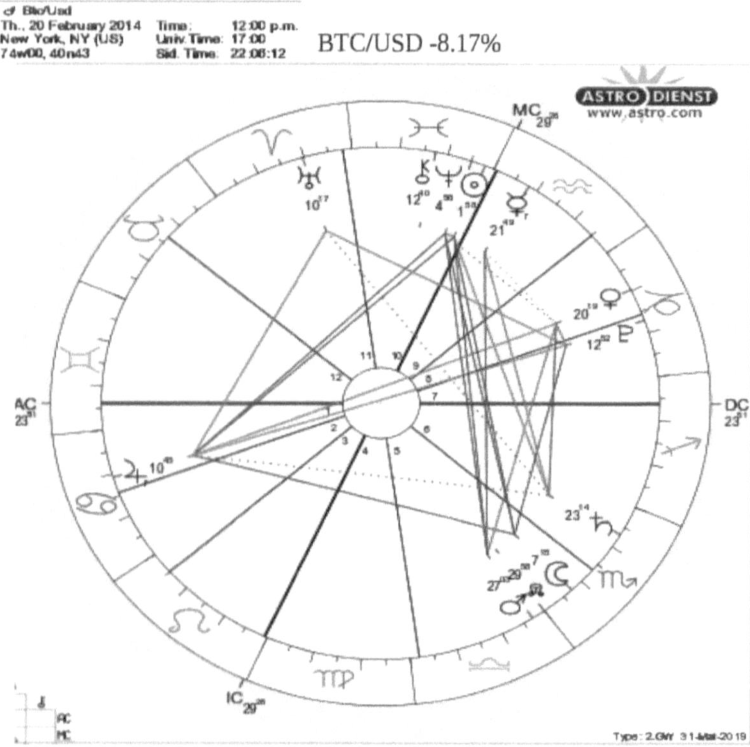

In this chart for Feb 20, 2014, Mercury's degree(21 degrees) higher than the sun's degree(1 degree). Therefore we continue with **"Figure Set 2"** parameters. The last parameter from **"Figure Set 2"** that would have applied here would be parameter 1, which says the moon being within 1 degree of the degree of the sun in an earth of water sign brings the value of BTC/USD down. That degree of the sun would be in Scorpio, which is a water sign. Therefore, the prediction is correct. BTC/USD was down -8.17%.

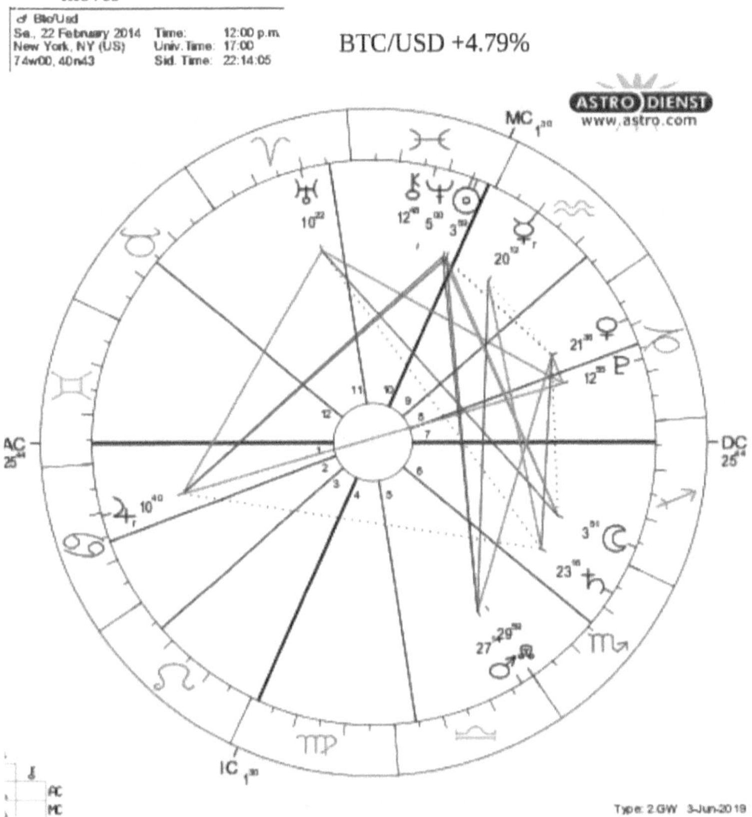

In this chart for Feb 22, 2014, Mercury's degree(20 degrees) is higher than the sun's degree(3 degree). Therefore we continue with "**Figure Set 2**" parameters. The last parameter from "**Figure Set 2**" that would have applied here would be parameter 2, which says the moon being within 1 degree of the degree of the sun in a fire or air sign brings the value of BTC/USD up. That degree of the sun would be in Sagittarius in this chart, which is a fire sign. Therefore, the prediction is correct. BTC/USD was up +4.79%.

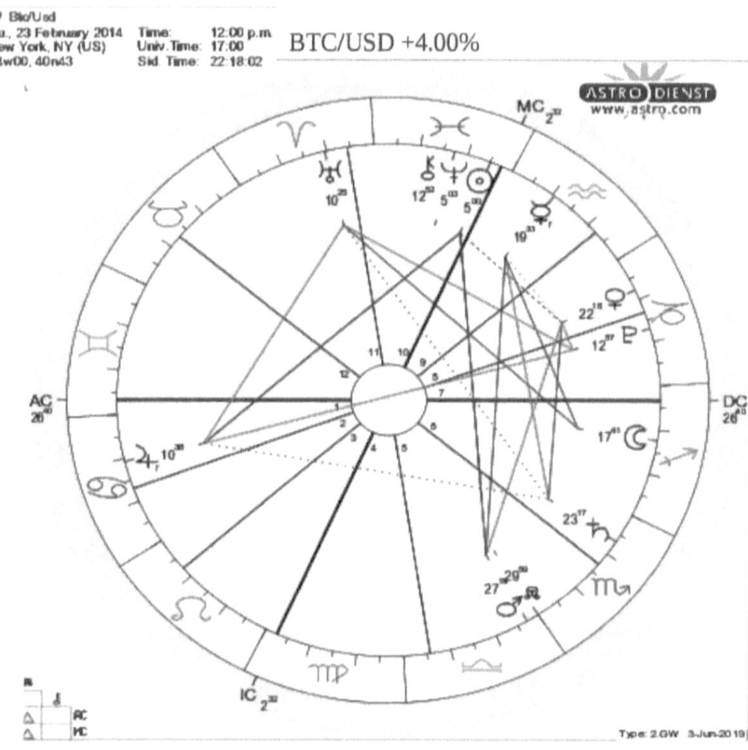

In this chart for Feb 23, 2014, Mercury's degree(19 degrees) higher than the sun's degree(5 degree). Therefore we continue with "**Figure Set 2**" parameters. The last parameter from "**Figure Set 2**" that would have applied here would be parameter 2 again, which says the moon being within 1 degree of the degree of the sun in a fire or air sign brings the value of BTC/USD up. That degree of the sun would be in Sagittarius in this chart, which is a fire sign. Therefore, the prediction is correct. BTC/ USD was up +4.00%.

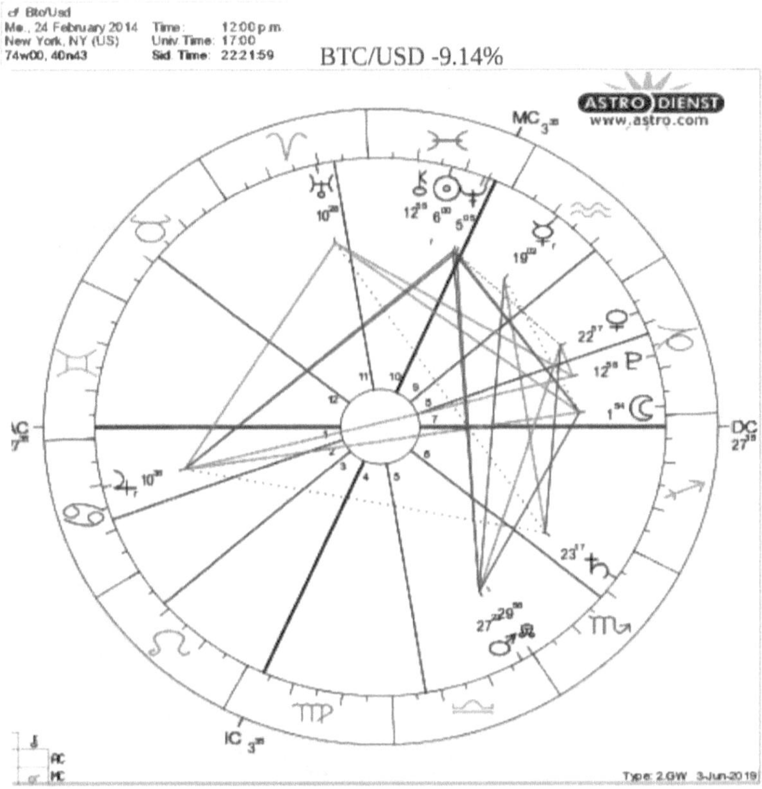

In this chart for Feb 24, 2014, Mercury's degree(19 degrees) higher than the sun's degree(6 degrees). Therefore we continue with **"Figure Set 2"** parameters. The last parameter from **"Figure Set 2"** that would have applied here would be parameter 5, which says the moon being within 1 degree of the degree of the lunar node after the moon has passed the sun's degree in an air or fire sign brings the value of BTC/ USD down. Before the moon went to within 1 degree of the degree of the lunar node in Capricorn, it had to last pass the degree of the sun in Sagittarius, which is a fire sign. Therefore, the prediction is correct. BTC/USD was down -9.14% this day.

In this chart for Feb 25, 2014, Mercury's degree(18 degrees) is higher than the sun's degree at (7 degrees). Therefore we continue with **"Figure Set 2"** parameters. The last parameter from **"Figure Set 2"** that would have applied here would be parameter 1, which says the moon being within 1 degree of the degree of the sun in an earth or water sign brings the value of BTC/USD down. That degree of the sun would have been in Capricorn because that's where the moon would have crossed it last. Capricorn is an earth sign. Therefore, the prediction is correct. BTC/USD was down -8.43% this day.

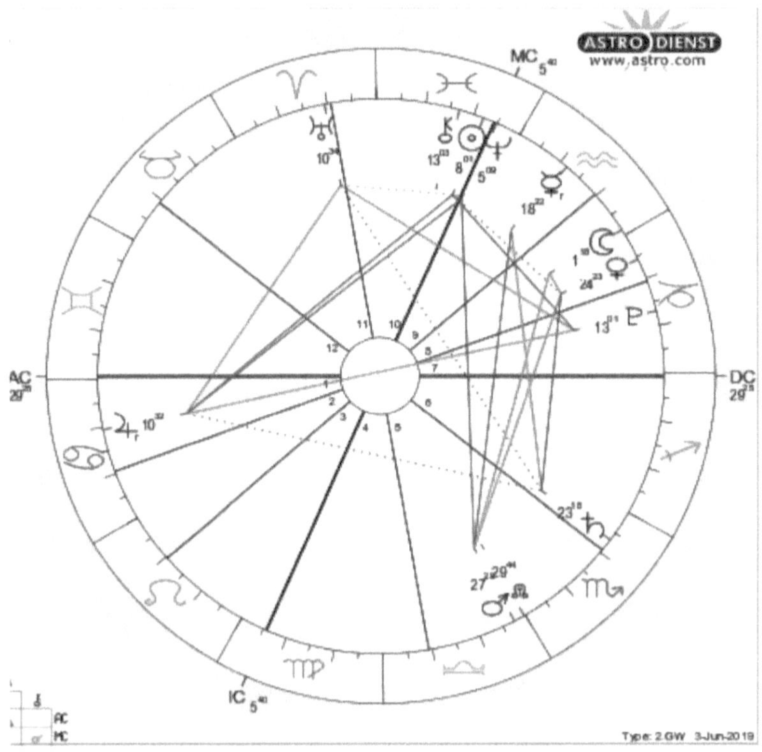

In this chart for Feb 26, 2014, Mercury's degree(18 degrees) is higher than the sun's degree(8 degrees). Therefore we continue with **"Figure Set 2"** parameters. The last parameter from **"Figure Set 2"** that would have applied here would be parameter 4, which says the moon being within 1 degree of the degree of the lunar node after the moon has passed the sun's degree in an earth or water sign brings the value of BTC/USD down. Before the moon went to within 1 degree of the degree of the lunar node in Aquarius, it had to last pass the degree of the sun in Capricorn, which is an earth sign. Therefore, the prediction is correct. BTC/USD was up +13.01% this day.

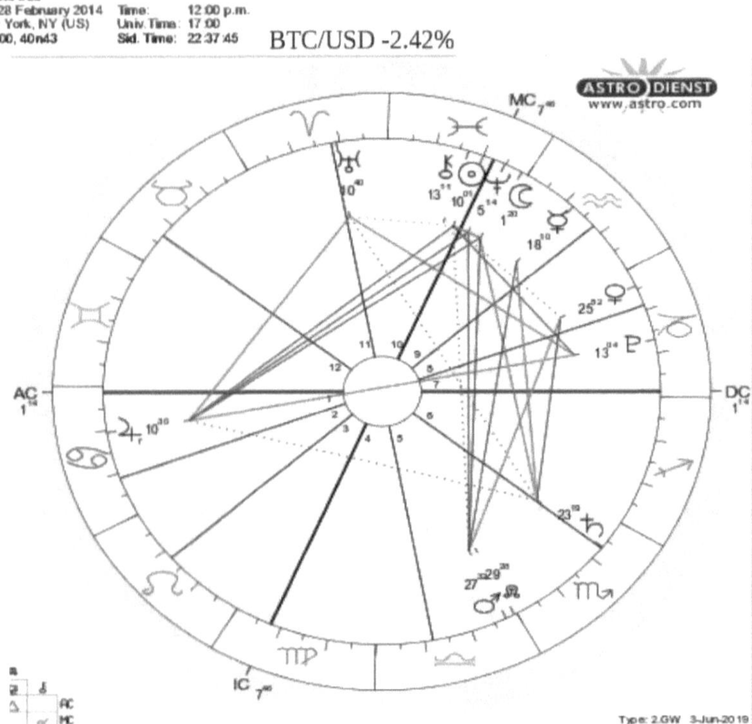

In this chart for Feb 28, 2014, Mercury's degree(18 degrees) is higher than the sun's degree(10 degrees). Therefore we continue with **"Figure Set 2"** parameters. The last parameter from **"Figure Set 2"** that would have applied here would be parameter 5, which says the moon being within 1 degree of the degree of the lunar node after the moon has passed the sun's degree in a fire or air sign brings the value of BTC/USD down. Before the moon went to within 1 degree of the degree of the lunar node in Pisces it had to last pass the degree of the sun in Aquarius, which is an air sign. Therefore, the prediction is correct. BTC/USD was down -2.42% this day.

These are the prices for the BTC/USD for the month of March 2014

Date	Price	Open	High	Low	Vol.	Change %	
Mar 31, 2014	452.0	478.6	485.0	443.1	0.08K	-2.61%	
Mar 30, 2014	464.1	493.0	493.0	440.4	0.14K	-5.66%	
Mar 29, 2014	491.9	506.2	507.0	491.0	0.02K	-1.11%	
Mar 28, 2014	497.4	525.0	525.0	490.0	0.23K	-0.22%	
Mar 27, 2014	498.5	582.4	589.3	498.5	0.24K	-16.21%	
Mar 26, 2014	595.0	580.0	595.0	570.0	0.54K	2.23%	
Mar 25, 2014	582.0	586.6	586.7	579.1	0.31K	-1.35%	
Mar 24, 2014	590.0	560.4	590.0	552.0	0.35K	4.20%	
Mar 23, 2014	566.2	570.3	570.3	566.2	0.01K	1.11%	
Mar 22, 2014	560.0	560.0	562.9	550.0	0.01K	-1.55%	
Mar 21, 2014	568.8	581.0	605.4	568.8	0.70K	-2.52%	
Mar 20, 2014	583.5	610.0	639.2	583.5	0.49K	-4.50%	
Mar 19, 2014	611.0	622.9	622.9	611.0	0.11K	-1.19%	
Mar 18, 2014	618.4	623.1	623.9	610.9	0.49K	-0.95%	
Mar 17, 2014	624.3	635.0	635.7	624.0	0.60K	-1.68%	
Mar 16, 2014	635.0	640.1	640.1	635.0	0.04K	-1.03%	
Mar 15, 2014	641.6	636.9	641.6	636.9	0.00K	1.85%	
Mar 14, 2014	630.0	632.9	639.0	630.0	0.56K	-1.87%	
Mar 13, 2014	642.0	633.5	645.1	633.5	0.04K	-1.23%	
Mar 12, 2014	650.0	615.0	650.0	615.0	0.86K	5.69%	
Mar 11, 2014	615.0	615.0	615.0	613.5	0.05K	0.00%	
Mar 10, 2014	615.0	621.0	621.0	612.8	0.12K	-0.97%	
Mar 09, 2014	621.0	610.5	621.0	609.4	0.05K	1.12%	
Mar 08, 2014	614.1	621.0	621.0	600.2	0.06K	-1.11%	
Mar 07, 2014	621.0	663.0	663.0	614.0	0.76K	-6.33%	
Mar 06, 2014	663.0	673.4	675.0	657.0	0.96K	-1.78%	
Mar 05, 2014	675.0	658.0	675.8	658.0	0.49K	1.05%	
Mar 04, 2014	668.0	654.7	675.0	652.6	0.47K	1.52%	
Mar 03, 2014	658.0	571.5	685.0	569.7	0.67K	17.37%	
Mar 02, 2014	560.6	570.9	583.5	560.0	0.01K	-1.34%	
Mar 01, 2014	568.2	565.0	571.8	560.0	0.06K	0.57%	

Change %: -20.0

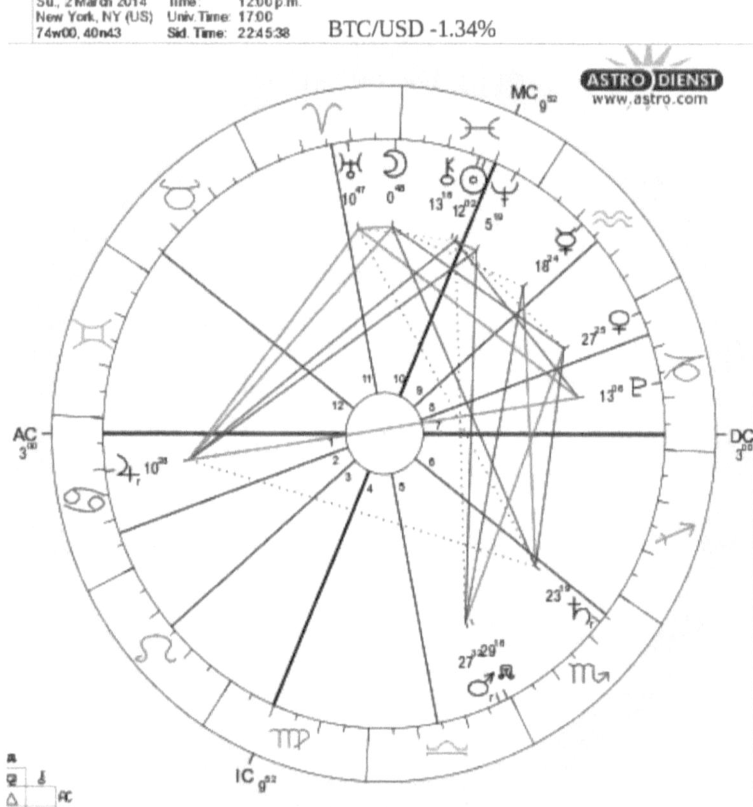

In this chart for Mar 2, 2014, Mercury's degree(18 degrees) is higher than the sun's degree(12 degrees). Therefore we continue with **"Figure Set 2"** parameters. The last parameter from **"Figure Set 2"** that would have applied here would be parameter 4, which says the moon being within 1 degree of the degree of the lunar node after the moon has passed the sun's degree in an earth or water sign brings the value of BTC/USD up. Before the moon went to within 1 degree of the degree of the lunar node in Aries it had to last pass the degree of the sun in Pisces, which is a water sign. Therefore, this prediction is WRONG. BTC/USD was down -1.34% this day.

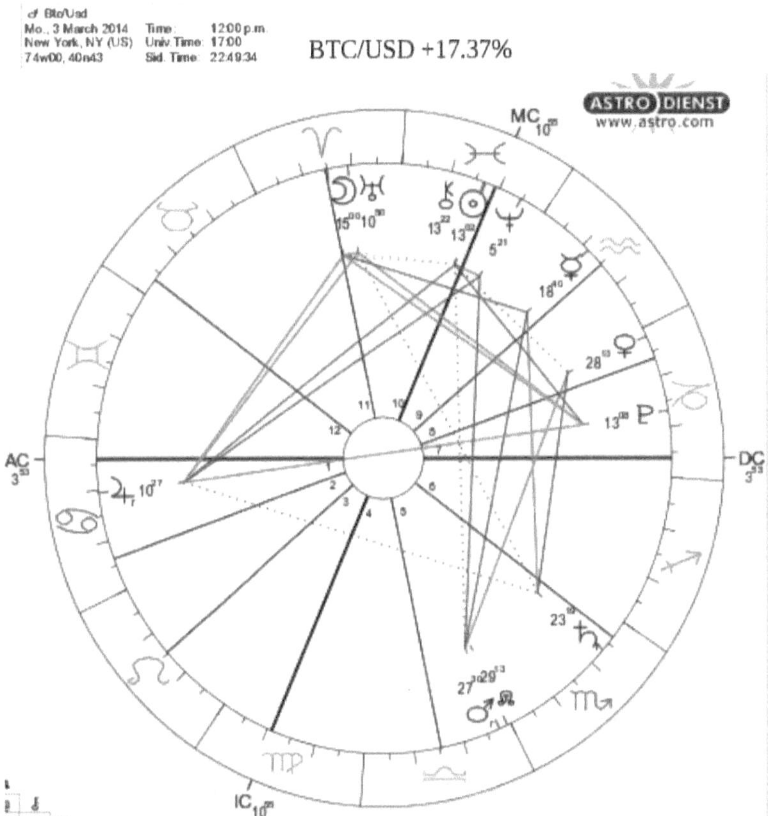

In this chart for Mar 3, 2014, Mercury's degree(18 degrees) is higher than the sun's degree(13 degrees). Therefore we continue with **"Figure Set 2"** parameters. The last parameter from **"Figure Set 2"** that would have applied here would be parameter 2, which says the moon being within 1 degree of the degree of the sun in an air or fire sign brings the value of BTC/USD up. That degree of the sun would be in Aries, which is a fire sign, Therefore, this prediction is CORRECT. BTC/USD was up +17.37% this day.

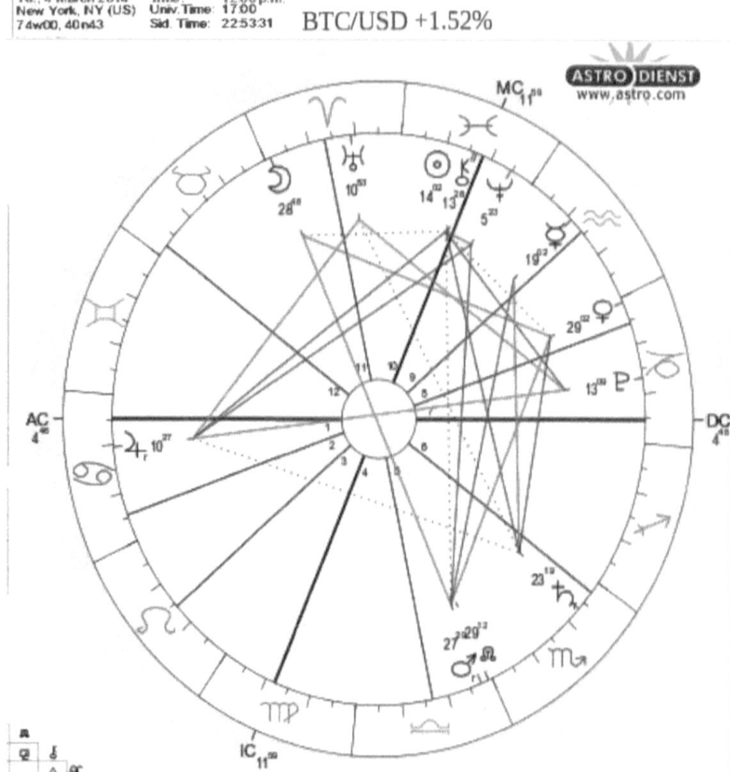

In this chart for Mar 4, 2014, Mercury's degree(19 degrees) is higher than the sun's degree(14 degrees). Therefore we continue with "**Figure Set 2**" parameters. The last parameter from "**Figure Set 2**" that would have applied here would be parameter 5, which says the moon being within 1 degree of the degree of the lunar node after the moon has passed the sun's degree in an air or fire sign brings the value of BTC/USD down. Before the moon went to within 1 degree of the degree of the lunar node in Taurus it had to last pass the degree of the sun in Aries, which is a fire sign. Therefore, this prediction is WRONG. BTC/USD was up +1.52% this day.

Starting March 6th, and continuing with the astro chart calculated for noon in New York, the algorithm that we have been using thus far for BTC/USD will taper off for a few days, as the next 3 major price moves for BTC/USD doesn't correlate with the algorithm. The price on March 6th when BTC/USD dropped -6.33%, the price on March 12th when BTC/USD rose +5.69%, and the price on March 24 when BTC/USD dropped -4.50% are all missed by the algorithm. Its not until March 25 that the algorithm recovers some accuracy and catches that next major price drop that takes place on March 27 , 2014, when the price of BTC/USD dropped -16.21%. Of course one can try to go back and make the algorithm fit by changing parameters around. However, a challenge to that would be keeping the algorithm historically relevant while doing so. When an algorithm tapers off for a few days, it doesn't mean that the algorithm no longer applies historically and vice versa an algorithm that works perfectly for 2 weeks doesn't mean that it will apply historically. There is a bit of game theory involved. Game theory is defined as "the branch of mathematics concerned with the analysis of strategies for dealing with competitive situations where the outcome of a participant's choice of action depends critically on the actions of other participants. Game theory has been applied to contexts in war, business, and biology." In the case of predictive analysis, if one algorithm allows one to be correct for a number of consecutive days but miss extremely important key dates historically or futuristically, then that has to be weighed against another algorithm that is less accurate in those same consecutive days, but at the same time more accurate historically and futuristically.

Applying that to what we have been using through the days in March in which our algorithm tapered of starting March 6th : if we continue with that same algorithm, despite that predictive slump, we eventually get to

March 25, where our algorithm recovers and catches the remaining key dates of BTC/USD price changes for the remainder of the month and also the next month of April. Had we tried to change the algorithm to make it fit more accurate in through that short term slump, we may have lost accuracy for those times the price moved significantly in the later days and weeks. Of course our example is related to an overall assessment of BTC/USD for the entire day. The parameters, however, allow for it to be used in real time. Meaning, one can use the algorithm to make predictions based on the exact time that the parameter applies. Since parameter 1 in **"Figure set 2"** says the moon within 1 degree of the degree of the sun in an earth or water sign brings the value of BTC/ USD down, one can calculate the chart to the exact time that happens and predict BTC/USD to start dropping at that time. This also applies for the algorithm in our EUR/USD example in Figure 1a and also our earlier Dow Jones example. I used what I felt applied most historically on key dates, but of course there is room for more analysis on this. There is much flexibility regarding how to apply the algorithm. I do believe, however, that using the Sun, Moon, Mercury and the Lunar node provides a fixed standard for daily prediction reliability over the course of time.

Below are percentage ups and downs of the BTC(Bitcoin)/USD currency pair during times when the Sun and Mercury are in the same sign and also during times when the Sun and Mercury are in different signs. These statistics go back to 2012. My initial observation would conclude that there is a higher prevalence of a rise in BTC/USD when the Sun and Mercury are in different signs and a higher prevalence of a drop when the Sun and Mercury are in the same sign. Mercury retrograde periods, however, seem to reverse that pattern, making it to where the Sun and Mercury in different signs would drive the BTC/USD lower, while the Sun and Mercury in the same sign (during the retrograde) would bring it higher. Any of the stats marked below with an asterisk * are the dates that would be affected by the mercury retrograde.

Here is the algorithm:

1. Sun and Mercury in a different sign = BTC/USD rises (unless there is a mercury retrograde which would then cause it to drop. Mercury retrograde times are marked with an asterisk)

2. Sun and Mercury in the same sign = BTC/USD drops(unless there is a mercury retrograde, which could then cause it to rise. Mercury retrograde times are marked with an asterisk)

Here are the stats staring back in 2012. Astrology charts calculated using western astrology, starting the beginning of a new sign at the 24th degree mark. The charts used to mark off the periods of when the Sun and Mercury are in the same sign and when they are in different signs were calculated for New York, Eastern Time Zone 11pm.

Sun & Mercury in the same sign
Feb 1, 2012 - Feb 9, 2012
BTC/USD down -4.1%

Sun & Mercury in different signs
Feb 10, 2012 - Feb 12, 2012
BTC/USD down -5.5%

Sun & Mercury in the same sign
Feb 13, 2012 - Feb 26, 2012
BTC/USD down -10.7%

Sun and Mercury in a different sign
Feb 27, 2012 - March 13, 2012
BTC/USD up +7.1%

(mercury retrograde Mar 12, 2012 - April 4, 2012)

Sun and Mercury in the same sign*
Mar 14, 2012 - Apr 1, 2012
BTC/USD down -8.3%

Sun and Mercury in a different sign
Apr 2, 2012 - Apr 5, 2012
BTC/USD up + 1.9%

Sun and Mercury in the same sign
Apr 6, 2012 - Apr 12, 2012
BTC/USD down -0.0%

Sun and Mercury in a different sign
Apr 13, 2012 - May 4, 2012
BTC/USD up + 3.0%

Sun and Mercury in the same sign
May 5, 2012 - May 13, 2012
BTC/USD down -2.8%

Sun and Mercury in a different sign
May 14, 2012 - May 20, 2012
BTC/USD up + 3.2%

Sun and Mercury in the same sign
May 21, 2012 - Jun 3, 2012
BTC/USD down +2.4%

Sun and Mercury in a different sign
Jun 4, 2012 - Jun 13, 2012
BTC/USD up +13.0%

Sun and Mercury in the same sign
Jun 14, 2012 - Jun 20, 2012
BTC/USD up +12.5%

Sun and Mercury in a different sign
Jun 21, 2012 - Jul 14, 2012
BTC/USD up +13.0%

(Mercury retrograde Jul 14 2012 - August 7, 2012)

Sun and Mercury in the same sign*
Jul 15, 2012 - Aug 15, 2012
BTC/USD up +75.7%

Sun and Mercury in a different sign
Aug 16, 2012 - Aug 27, 2012
BTC/USD down -17.4%

Sun and Mercury in the same sign
Aug 28, 2012 - Sep 12, 2012
BTC/USD up +3.7%

Sun and Mercury in a different sign
Sep 13, 2012 - Sep 15, 2012
BTC/USD up +3.4%

Sun and Mercury in the same sign
Sep 16, 2012 - Sep 30, 2012
BTC/USD up +5.5%

Sun and Mercury in a different sign
Oct 1, 2012 - Oct 15, 2012
BTC/USD down -4.5%

Sun and Mercury in the same sign
Oct 16, 2012 - Oct 22, 2012
BTC/USD down -1.1%

(Mercury retrograde Nov 6 2012 - Nov 26, 2012)

Sun and Mercury in a different sign*
Oct 23, 2012 - Nov 14, 2012
BTC/USD down -6.5%

Sun and Mercury in the same sign*
Nov 15, 2012 - Nov 17, 2012
BTC/USD up +7.7%

Sun and Mercury in a different sign*
Nov 18, 2012 - Dec 4, 2012
BTC/USD up +13.7%

Sun and Mercury in the same sign
Dec 5, 2012 - Dec 14, 2012
BTC/USD up +1.4%

Sun and Mercury in a different sign
Dec 15, 2012 - Dec 26, 2012
BTC/USD down -1.0%

Sun and Mercury in the same sign
Dec 26, 2012 - Jan 12, 2013
BTC/USD up +5.7%

Sun and Mercury in a different sign
Jan 13, 2013 - Jan 14, 2013
BTC/USD up +0.4%

Sun and Mercury in the same sign
Jan 13, 2013 - Jan 31, 2013
BTC/USD up +42.7%

Sun and Mercury in a different sign
Feb 1, 2013 - Feb 11, 2013
BTC/USD up +20.0%

(mercury retrograde February 23, 2013 - March 17, 2013)

Sun and Mercury in the same sign*
Feb 12, 2013 - Mar 13, 2013
BTC/USD up +90.3%

Sun and Mercury in a different sign
Mar 14, 2013 - Apr 8, 2013
BTC/USD up +299.0%

Sun and Mercury in the same sign
Apr 9, 2013 - Apr 13, 2013
BTC/USD down -50.3%

Sun and Mercury in a different sign
Apr 14, 2013 - Apr 27, 2013
BTC/USD up +37.0%

Sun and Mercury in the same sign
Apr 28, 2013 - May 11, 2013
BTC/USD down -9.7%

Sun and Mercury in a different sign
May 12, 2013 - May 13, 2013
BTC/USD up +2.0%

Sun and Mercury in the same sign
May 14, 2013 - May 26, 2013
BTC/USD up +13.2%

Sun and Mercury in a different sign
May 27, 2013 - Jun 13, 2013
BTC/USD down -22.1%

(Mercury retrograde June 26, 2013 - July 20, 2013)

Sun and Mercury in the same sign*
Jun 14, 2013 - Jul 15, 2013
BTC/USD up -10.4%

Sun and Mercury in a different sign
Jul 16, 2013 - Aug 3, 2013
BTC/USD up +3.8%

Sun and Mercury in the same sign
Aug 4, 2013 - Aug 15, 2013
BTC/USD up +0.9%

Sun and Mercury in a different sign
Aug 16, 2013 - Aug 19, 2013
BTC/USD up +4.9%

Sun and Mercury in the same sign
Aug 20, 2013 - Sep 4, 2013
BTC/USD up +17.9%

Sun and Mercury in a different sign
Sep 5, 2013 - Sep 15, 2013
BTC/USD up +3.3%

Sun and Mercury in the same sign
Sep 16, 2013 - Sep 23, 2013
BTC/USD down -1.9%

Sun and Mercury in a different sign
Sep 24, 2013 - Oct 16, 2013
BTC/USD up +12.4%

(Mercury retrograde October 21 2013 - November 10, 2013)

Sun and Mercury in the same sign*
Oct 17, 2013 - Nov 15, 2013
BTC/USD up +191.1%

Sun and Mercury in a different sign
Nov 16, 2013 - Nov 29, 2013
BTC/USD up +176.4%

Sun and Mercury in the same sign
Nov 30, 2013 - Dec 14, 2013
BTC/USD down -19.3%

Sun and Mercury in a different sign
Dec 15, 2013 - Dec 19, 2013
BTC/USD down -21.8%

Sun and Mercury in the same sign
Dec 20, 2013 - Jan 7, 2014
BTC/USD up +12.7%

Sun and Mercury in a different sign
Jan 8, 2014 - Jan 13, 2014
BTC/USD up +3.5%

Sun and Mercury in the same sign
Jan 14, 2014 - Jan 25, 2014
BTC/USD down -1.0%

(mercury retrograde Feb 6, 2014 - Feb 28, 2014)

Sun and Mercury in a different sign*
Jan 26, 2014 - Feb 11, 2014
BTC/USD down -18.7%

Sun and Mercury in the same sign*
Feb 12, 2014 - Feb 17, 2014
BTC/USD up +0.8%

Sun and Mercury in a different sign*
Feb 18, 2014 - Mar 10, 2014
BTC/USD down -7.4%

Sun and Mercury in the same sign
Mar 11, 2014 - Mar 13, 2014
BTC/USD up +4.4%

Sun and Mercury in a different sign
Mar 14, 2014 - Apr 2, 2014
BTC/USD down -30.9%

Sun and Mercury in the same sign
Apr 3, 2014 - Apr 12, 2014
BTC/USD down -6.4%

Sun and Mercury in a different sign
Apr 13, 2014 - Apr 19, 2014
BTC/USD up +21.7%

Sun and Mercury in the same sign
Apr 20, 2014 - May 3, 2014
BTC/USD down -12.8%

Sun and Mercury in a different sign
May 4, 2014 - May 13, 2014
BTC/USD up +21.7%

Sun and Mercury in the same sign
May 14, 2014 - May 21, 2014
BTC/USD up +9.2%

Sun and Mercury in a different sign
May 22, 2014 - Jun 14, 2014
BTC/USD up +16.7%

(Mercury retrograde June 7, 2012 - July 1, 2012)

Sun and Mercury in the same sign*
Jun 15, 2014 - Jul 15, 2014
BTC/USD up +12.0%

Sun and Mercury in a different sign
Jul 16, 2014 - Jul 27, 2014
BTC/USD down -4.9%

Sun and Mercury in the same sign
Jul 28, 2014 - Aug 11, 2014
BTC/USD down -3.0%

Sun and Mercury in a different sign
Aug 12, 2014 - Aug 15, 2014
BTC/USD down -11.6%

Sun and Mercury in the same sign
Aug 16, 2014 - Aug 28, 2014
BTC/USD up +0.3%

Sun and Mercury in a different sign

Aug 29, 2014 - Sept 15, 2014
BTC/USD down -7.5%

Sun and Mercury in the same sign
Sep 16, 2014 - Sep 19, 2014
BTC/USD down -15.9%

(Mercury Retrograde October 4, 2014 - October 25, 2014)

Sun and Mercury in a different sign*
Sep 20, 2014 - Oct 15, 2014
BTC/USD down -0.5%

Sun and Mercury in the same sign*
Oct 16, 2014
BTC/USD down -3.6%

Sun and Mercury in a different sign*
Oct 17, 2014 - Nov 3, 2014
BTC/USD down -14.7%

Sun and Mercury in the same sign
Nov 4, 2014 - Nov 15, 2014
BTC/USD up +16.4%

Sun and Mercury in a different sign
Nov 16, 2014 - Nov 23, 2014
BTC/USD down -4.2%

Sun and Mercury in the same sign
Nov 24, 2014 - Dec 12, 2014
BTC/USD down -2.1%

Sun and Mercury in a different sign
Dec 13, 2014 - Dec 14, 2014
BTC/USD down 0.0%

Sun and Mercury in the same sign
Dec 14, 2014 - Dec 31, 2014
BTC/USD down -10.1%

Sun and Mercury in a different sign
Jan 1, 2015 - Jan 13, 2015
BTC/USD down -27.5%

(Mercury retrograde Jan 21, 2015 - February 11, 2015)

Sun and Mercury in the same sign*
Jan 14, 2015 - Feb 11, 2015
BTC/USD down -4.4%

Sun and Mercury in a different sign
Feb 12, 2015 - Mar 7, 2015
BTC/USD up +26.0%

Sun and Mercury in the same sign
Mar 8, 2015 - Mar 13, 2015
BTC/USD up +2.3%

Sun and Mercury in a different sign
Mar 14, 2015 - Mar 26, 2015
BTC/USD down -12.0%

Sun and Mercury in the same sign
Mar 27, 2015 - Apr 11, 2015
BTC/USD down -4.9%

Sun and Mercury in a different sign
Apr 12, 2015 - Apr 13, 2015
BTC/USD down -5.0%

Sun and Mercury in the same sign
Apr 14, 2015 - Apr 26, 2015
BTC/USD down -2.4%

Sun and Mercury in a different sign
Apr 27, 2015 - May 14, 2015
BTC/USD up +7.7%

(Mercury retrograde May 18, 2015 - June 11, 2015)

Sun and Mercury in the same sign*
May 15, 2015 - Jun 14, 2015
BTC/USD down -1.3%

Sun and Mercury in a different sign
Jun 15, 2015 - Jul 4, 2015
BTC/USD up +11.6%

Sun and Mercury in the same sign*
Jul 5, 2015 - Jun 15, 2015
BTC/USD up +9.5%

Sun and Mercury in a different sign

Jul 16, 2015 - Jul 19, 2015
BTC/USD down -3.6%

Sun and Mercury in the same sign
Jul 20, 2015 - Aug 3, 2015
BTC/USD up +2.3%

Sun and Mercury in a different sign
Aug 4, 2015 - Aug 16, 2015
BTC/USD down -7.6%

Sun and Mercury in the same sign
Aug 17, 2015 - Aug 21, 2015
BTC/USD down -10.7%

Sun and Mercury in a different sign
Aug 22, 2015 - Sep 16, 2015
BTC/USD down -1.4%

(Mercury retrograde September 17, 2015 - October 9 2015)

Sun and Mercury in the same sign*
Sep 17, 2015 - Oct 16, 2015
BTC/USD up +15.7%

Sun and Mercury in a different sign
Oct 17, 2015 - Oct 28, 2015
BTC/USD up +15.6%

Sun and Mercury in the same sign
Oct 29, 2015 - Dec 5, 2015
BTC/USD up +28.1%

Sun and Mercury in a different sign
Dec 6, 2015 - Dec 15, 2015
BTC/USD up +19.6%

Sun and Mercury in the same sign
Dec 16, 2015 - Dec 25, 2015
BTC/USD down -2.4%

Mercury retrograde January 5th, 2016 – January 25th, 2016)

Sun and Mercury in a different sign*
Dec 26, 2015 - Feb 7, 2016
BTC/USD down -18.3%

Sun and Mercury in the same sign
Feb 8, 2016 - Feb 12, 2016
BTC/USD up +2.9%

Sun and Mercury in a different sign
Feb 13, 2016 - Feb 29, 2016
BTC/USD up +14.7%

Sun and Mercury in the same sign
Mar 1, 2016 - Mar 13, 2016
BTC/USD down -6.2%

Sun and Mercury in a different sign
Mar 14, 2016 - Mar 17, 2016
BTC/USD up +1.7%

Sun and Mercury in the same sign
Mar 18, 2016 - Apr 1, 2016
BTC/USD down -0.3%

Sun and Mercury in a different sign
Apr 2, 2016 - Apr 12, 2016
BTC/USD up +2.2%

(Mercury Retrograde April 28th 2016 – May 22nd, 2016)

Sun and Mercury in the same sign*
Apr 13, 2016 - May 13, 2016
BTC/USD up +6.8%

Sun and Mercury in a different sign
May 13, 2016 - Jun 6, 2016
BTC/USD up +28.4%

Sun and Mercury in the same sign
Jun 7, 2016 - Jun 13, 2016
BTC/USD up +20.6%

Sun and Mercury in a different sign
Jun 14, 2016 - Jun 25, 2016
BTC/USD down -5.8%

Sun and Mercury in the same sign
Jun 26, 2016 - Jul 10, 2016
BTC/USD down -2.3%

Sun and Mercury in a different sign

Jul 11, 2016 - Jul 14, 2016
BTC/USD up +1.5%

Sun and Mercury in the same sign
Jul 15, 2016 - Jul 25, 2016
BTC/USD down -0.9%

Sun and Mercury in a different sign
Jul 26, 2016 - Aug 15, 2016
BTC/USD down -13.7%

Sun and Mercury in the same sign
Aug 16, 2016 - Aug 18, 2016
BTC/USD up +1.3%

Sun and Mercury in a different sign
Aug 19, 2016 - Sep 8, 2016
BTC/USD up +10.4%

(Mercury retrograde August 30, 2016 - September 22, 2016)

Sun and Mercury in the same sign*
Sep 9, 2016 - Sep 15, 2016
BTC/USD down -3.2%

Sun and Mercury in a different sign
Sep 16, 2016 - Oct 2, 2016
BTC/USD down -0.4%

Sun and Mercury in the same sign
Oct 3, 2016 - Oct 15, 2016
BTC/USD up +5.1%

Sun and Mercury in a different sign
Oct 16, 2016 - Oct 20, 2016
BTC/USD down -1.2%

Sun and Mercury in the same sign
Oct 21, 2016 - Nov 7, 2016
BTC/USD up +11.3%

Sun and Mercury in a different sign
Nov 9, 2016 - Nov 14, 2016
BTC/USD up +0.47%

Sun and Mercury in the same sign
Nov 15, 2016 - Nov 27, 2016

BTC/USD up +2.5%

Sun and Mercury in a different sign
Nov 28, 2016 - Dec 14, 2016
BTC/USD up +6.08%

(Mercury retrograde December 19th, 2016 – January 8th, 2017)

Sun and Mercury in the same sign*
Dec 15, 2016 - Jan 12, 2017
BTC/USD up +3.9%

Sun and Mercury in a different sign
Jan 13, 2017 - Feb 2, 2017
BTC/USD up +25.0%

Sun and Mercury in the same sign
Feb 3, 2017 - Feb 11, 2017
BTC/USD down -0.5%

Sun and Mercury in a different sign
Feb 12, 2017 - Feb 21, 2017
BTC/USD up +12.9%

Sun and Mercury in the same sign
Feb 22, 2017 - Mar 9, 2017
BTC/USD up +5.4%

Sun and Mercury in a different sign
Mar 10, 2017 - Mar 13, 2017
BTC/USD up +4.0%

Sun and Mercury in the same sign
Mar 14, 2017 - Mar 25, 2017
BTC/USD down -21.5%

Sun and Mercury in a different sign
Mar 26, 2017 - Apr 12, 2017
BTC/USD up +26.3%

(Mercury retrograde April 9, 2017 - May 3, 2017)

Sun and Mercury in the same sign*
Apr 13, 2017 - May 13, 2017
BTC/USD up +48.3%

Sun and Mercury in a different sign

May 14, 2017 - Jun 2, 2017
BTC/USD up +32.3%

Sun and Mercury in the same sign
Jun 3, 2017 - Jun 13, 2017
BTC/USD up +11.2%

Sun and Mercury in a different sign
Jun 14, 2017 - Jun 17, 2017
BTC/USD down -2.5%

Sun and Mercury in the same sign
Jun 18, 2017 - Jul 1, 2017
BTC/USD down -10.0%

Sun and Mercury in a different sign
Jul 2, 2017 - Jul 15, 2017
BTC/USD down -15.8%

Sun and Mercury in the same sign
Jul 16, 2017 - Jul 19, 2017
BTC/USD up +13.9%

Sun and Mercury in a different sign
Jul 20, 2017 - Aug 15, 2017
BTC/USD up +84.3%

(Mercury retrograde August 12, 2017 - September 5, 2017)

Sun and Mercury in the same sign*
Aug 16, 2017 - Sep 15, 2017
BTC/USD down -10.9%

Sun and Mercury in a different sign
Sep 16, 2017 - Sep 25, 2017
BTC/USD up +6.3%

Sun and Mercury in the same sign
Sep 26, 2017 - Oct 12, 2017
BTC/USD up +38.1%

Sun and Mercury in a different sign
Oct 13, 2017 - Oct 16, 2017
BTC/USD up +6.2%

Sun and Mercury in the same sign
Oct 17, 2017 - Oct 31, 2017

BTC/USD up +12.1%

Sun and Mercury in a different sign
Nov 1, 2017 - Nov 15, 2017
BTC/USD up +12.7%

Sun and Mercury in the same sign
Nov 16, 2017 - Nov 23, 2017
BTC/USD up +9.6%

Sun and Mercury in a different sign
Nov 23, 2017 - Dec 9, 2017
BTC/USD up +83.8%

(Mercury retrograde December 3 - December 22, 2017)

Sun and Mercury in the same sign*
Dec 10, 2017 - Dec 14, 2017
BTC/USD up +11.8%

Sun and Mercury in a different sign
Dec 15, 2017 - Jan 5, 2018
BTC/USD up +3.3%

Sun and Mercury in the same sign
Jan 6, 2018 - Jan 13, 2018
BTC/USD down -16.1%

Sun and Mercury in a different sign
Jan 14, 2018 - Jan 26, 2018
BTC/USD down -22.0%

Sun and Mercury in the same sign
Jan 27, 2018 - Feb 11, 2018
BTC/USD down -27.1%

Sun and Mercury in a different sign
Feb 12, 2018 - Feb 13, 2018
BTC/USD up +5.5%

Sun and Mercury in the same sign
Feb 14, 2018 - Mar 1, 2018
BTC/USD up +28.3%

Sun and Mercury in a different sign
Mar 2, 2018 - Mar 13, 2018
BTC/USD down -16.4%

(Mercury retrograde March 22 - April 15, 2018)

Sun and Mercury in the same sign*
Mar 14, 2018 - Apr 12, 2018
BTC/USD down -13.4%

Sun and Mercury in a different sign
Apr 13, 2018 - May 8, 2018
BTC/USD up +16.1%

Sun and Mercury in the same sign
May 9, 2018 - May 13, 2018
BTC/USD down -5.5%

Sun and Mercury in a different sign
May 14, 2018 - May 25, 2018
BTC/USD down -14.1%

Sun and Mercury in the same sign
May 26, 2018 - Jun 8, 2018
BTC/USD up +2.1%

Sun and Mercury in a different sign
Jun 9, 2018 - Jun 14, 2018
BTC/USD down -12.9%

Sun and Mercury in the same sign
Jun 15, 2018 - Jun 24, 2018
BTC/USD down -7.3%

Sun and Mercury in a different sign
Jun 25, 2018 - Jul 15, 2018
BTC/USD up +3.2%

(Mercury retrograde July 25, 2018 - August 18, 2018)

Sun and Mercury in the same sign*
Jul 16, 2018 - Aug 15, 2018
BTC/USD down -1.2%

Sun and Mercury in a different sign
Aug 16, 2018 - Sep 1, 2018
BTC/USD up +14.8%

Sun and Mercury in the same sign
Sep 2, 2018 - Sep 15, 2018

BTC/USD down -9.5%

Sun and Mercury in a different sign
Sep 16, 2018 - Sep 17, 2018
BTC/USD down -4.0%

Sun and Mercury in the same sign
Sep 18, 2018 - Oct 5, 2018
BTC/USD up +6.2%

Sun and Mercury in a different sign
Oct 6, 2018 - Oct 16, 2018
BTC/USD up +1.6%

Sun and Mercury in the same sign
Oct 17, 2018 - Oct 25, 2018
BTC/USD down -3.3%

Sun and Mercury in a different sign
Oct 26, 2018 - Nov 15, 2018
BTC/USD down -11.9%

(Mercury retrograde November 16, 2018 - December 06, 2018)

Sun and Mercury in the same sign*
Nov 16, 2018 - Dec 14, 2018
BTC/USD down -42.8%

Sun and Mercury in a different sign
Dec 15, 2018 - Dec 30, 2018
BTC/USD up +21.2%

Sun and Mercury in the same sign
Dec 31, 2018 - Jan 13, 2019
BTC/USD down -9.7%

Sun and Mercury in a different sign
Jan 14, 2019 - Jan 19, 2019
BTC/USD up +4.7%

Sun and Mercury in the same sign
Jan 20, 2019 - Feb 5, 2019
BTC/USD down -6.6%

Sun and Mercury in a different sign
Feb 6, 2019 - Feb 11, 2019
BTC/USD up +4.8%

Sun and Mercury in the same sign
Feb 12, 2019 - Feb 23, 2019
BTC/USD up +14.4%

(Mercury retrograde March 5, 2019 to March 28, 2019)

Sun and Mercury in a different sign*
Feb 24, 2019 - Mar 13, 2019
BTC/USD down -6.3%

Sun and Mercury in the same sign*
Mar 14, 2019
BTC/USD up +0.0%

Sun and Mercury in a different sign
Mar 15, 2019 - Apr 10, 2019
BTC/USD up +34.5%

Sun and Mercury in the same sign
Apr 11, 2019 - Apr 13, 2019
BTC/USD down -4.0%

Sun and Mercury in a different sign
Apr 14, 2019 - May 2, 2019
BTC/USD up +12.2%

Sun and Mercury in the same sign
Apr 11, 2019 - Apr 13, 2019
BTC/USD up +35.5%

Sun and Mercury in a different sign
May 14, 2019 - May 17, 2019
BTC/USD down -4.4%

Sun and Mercury in the same sign
May 18, 2019 - May 31, 2019
BTC/USD up +15.1%

Sun and Mercury in a different sign
Jun 1, 2019 - Jun 14, 2019
BTC/USD up +1.8%

Sun and Mercury in the same sign
Jun 15, 2019 - Jun 19, 2019
BTC/USD up +15.1%

Sun and Mercury in a different sign
Jun 20, 2019 - Jul 15, 2019
BTC/USD up +16.3%

(Mercury retrograde July 7, 2019 to August 2, 2019)

Sun and Mercury in the same sign*
Jul 16, 2019 - Jul 30, 2019
BTC/USD down -11.4%

Sun and Mercury in a different sign*
Jul 31, 2019 - Aug 1, 2019
BTC/USD up +8.4%

Sun and Mercury in the same sign
Aug 2, 2019 - Aug 16, 2019
BTC/USD down -0.3%

Sun and Mercury in a different sign
Aug 17, 2019 - Aug 25, 2019
BTC/USD down -2.3%

Sun and Mercury in the same sign
Aug 26, 2019 - Sep 9, 2019
BTC/USD up +1.8%

Sun and Mercury in a different sign
Sep 10, 2019 - Sep 16, 2019
BTC/USD down -0.2%

Sun and Mercury in the same sign
Sep 17, 2019 - Sep 28, 2019
BTC/USD down -20.0%

Sun and Mercury in a different sign
Sep 29, 2019 - Oct 16, 2019
BTC/USD down -0.2%

Sun and Mercury in the same sign
Oct 17, 2019 - Oct 22, 2019
BTC/USD up +0.5%

Sun and Mercury in a different sign
Oct 23, 2019 - Nov 6, 2019
BTC/USD up +16.1%

(Mercury retrograde October 31 2019 to November 20 2019)

Sun and Mercury in the same sign*
Nov 7, 2019 - Nov 15, 2019
BTC/USD down -9.2%

Sun and Mercury in a different sign
Nov 16, 2019 - Dec 3, 2019
BTC/USD down -13.7%

Sun and Mercury in the same sign
Dec, 4 2019 - Dec 15, 2019
BTC/USD down -2.5%

Sun and Mercury in a different sign
Dec 16, 2019 - Dec 24, 2019
BTC/USD up +1.7%

Sun and Mercury in the same sign
Dec, 25 2019 - Jan 11, 2020
BTC/USD up +10.4%

--------------------------Results of algorithm for the year 2020------------------------

Sun and Mercury in a different sign
Jan, 12 2020 - Jan 14, 2020
BTC/USD up +10.0%

Sun and Mercury in the same sign
Jan, 15 2020 - Jan 29, 2020
BTC/USD up +5.3%

Sun and Mercury in a different sign
Jan 30, 2020 - Feb 12, 2020
BTC/USD up +11.0%

(Mercury retrograde Februrary 18 2020 to March 9 2020)

Sun and Mercury in the same sign*
Feb 13, 2020 - Mar 13, 2020
BTC/USD down -45.9%
please note that BTC/USD dropped 38.18% on March 12th after mercury retrograde already ended.

Sun and Mercury in a different sign
Mar 14, 2020 - Apr 7, 2020
BTC/USD up +28.0%

Sun and Mercury in the same sign
Apr 8, 2020 - Apr 13, 2020
BTC/USD down -4.8%

Sun and Mercury in a different sign
Apr 14, 2020 - Apr 24, 2020
BTC/USD up +9.7%

Sun and Mercury in the same sign
Apr 25, 2020 - May 8, 2020
BTC/USD up +30.5%

Sun and Mercury in a different sign
May 9, 2020 - May 13, 2020
BTC/USD down -5.2%

Sun and Mercury in the same sign
May 14, 2020 - May 23, 2020
BTC/USD down -1.3%

Sun and Mercury in a different sign
May 24, 2020 - Jun 13, 2020
BTC/USD up +3.2%

(Mercury retrograde Jun 18 2020 to Jul 11 2020)

Sun and Mercury in the same sign*
Jun 14, 2020 - Jul 15, 2020
BTC/USD down -2.9%

Sun and Mercury in a different sign
Jul 16, 2020 - Jul 31, 2020
BTC/USD up +23.2%

Sun and Mercury in the same sign
Aug 1, 2020 - Aug 15, 2020
BTC/USD up +4.5%

Sun and Mercury in a different sign
Aug 16, 2020 - Aug 16, 2020
BTC/USD up +0.5%

Sun and Mercury in the same sign
Aug 17, 2020 - Sep 1, 2020
BTC/USD up +0.1%

Sun and Mercury in a different sign
Sep 2, 2020 - Sep 15, 2020
BTC/USD down -9.5%

Sun and Mercury in the same sign
Sep 16, 2020 - Sep 21, 2020
BTC/USD down -3.4%

Sun and Mercury in a different sign
Sep 22, 2020 - Oct 15, 2020
BTC/USD up +10.4%

(Mercury retrograde Oct 14, 2020 to Nov 3 2020)

Sun and Mercury in the same sign*
Oct 16, 2020 - Nov 14, 2020
BTC/USD up +39.4%

Sun and Mercury in a different sign
Nov 15, 2020 - Nov 26, 2020
BTC/USD up +7.2%

Sun and Mercury in the same sign
Nov 26, 2020 - Dec 14, 2020
BTC/USD BTC/USD up +2.9%

Sun and Mercury in a different sign
Dec 15, 2020 - Dec 16, 2020
BTC/USD BTC/USD up +10.6%